THE KEYS TO PROLIFIC CREATIVITY

By

David V. Stewart

Contents

The Keys to Prolific Creativity

Introduction: On Being Prolific

What does it mean to actually be prolific?

Usually, it means that someone is outputting a great deal of something: a prolific writer, a prolific musician, a prolific painter, etc. puts out a lot of work in their area of expertise.

I'm a bit different, though, in that I tend to split my productivity among several pursuits: writing books, writing blog content, recording informative (and hopefully somewhat entertaining) videos, recording music, and raising children.

Yes, we often do not think of raising children as part of productivity, but it certainly is. Your progeny is in many ways your biggest legacy, and is also one of the biggest contributions you can make to your culture, yet children are often pushed to the side when considering accomplishments.

What do children have to do with being prolific in art? A great deal, as you shall see. Productivity is a balancing act. You can only do so much in a given day, and the pursuit of being prolific means maximizing the time that you have available to you. Family, work, and other life obligations are going to take some of that time.

To that end, there are nine guiding ideas – nine "keys" if you will – that I have found immensely helpful in being creatively productive and prolifically creative. Here is a general overview of each one, before we get deep into understanding them and applying them.

1. Align Your Priorities

And so, the first step to achieving a prolific work output is to properly align your priorities. I've learned through a great deal of personal growth and struggle that the dissonance that sucks the creativity out of your will is mostly born in the misalignment of priorities. Ignoring health or family will not only suck the enjoyment out of your accomplishments, it will also be an impediment to your process as you will not be emotionally and physically able to do engage with your creative self and put in the hard work necessary to bring projects to fruition.

2. Establish a Creative Process

Once you establish your priorities, you can work on your creative process, knowing what limitations you have in terms of time and energy. Creative processes vary by person, but the usual goal is efficiency and effectiveness, and discovering how to have both of these things is largely an individual pursuit as well as a process unto itself.

In other words, part of the creative process is refining your creative process. A creative process is generally a set of procedures you use to produce output and move a project closer to completion. For writers, this is usually a daily word count goal; for musicians, it is usually a daily practice session. However, I can tell you as both an experienced music instructor and a writing coach that how one goes about these two things can vary wildly.

One person needs to outline a book heavily in order to write anything, others will find outlining to be anti-creative and suck the fun out of the drafting process entirely. Likewise, when practicing a musical instrument how one goes about practicing can vary – one person needs extensive technique warmups, another not only does not need them, he will have no energy to practice unless he can avoid repetitive exercises and spend his time solely on practicing repertoire – or composing original music.

3. Establish Effective Goals

The next step is to establish effective goals. If you think that should come first, you are partially right. Again, it depends on one's mindset. Some people are very energized by goals, but I have found that processes are much more powerful than goals. An effective routine will persist even if a goal proves untenable or a completed project ends up being a failure.

Nevertheless, goals are still important, as one wants to be working with some express purpose in mind. Establishing effective goals means more than just making a "wish," like saying to oneself, "I want to be a writer." Goals need to be time-bound, specific, and properly aligned with the creative process.

For example, if you are able to consistently write one thousand words a day, you can easily figure out how long it will take you to write a book of a certain length. A hundred-thousand-word book will take you a minimum of 100 days, so an effective goal would be "I'm going to finish this book by May 10th," if you are setting the goal on January first.

Music and art goals will have their own timelines, depending on the goal. One thing you can expect as you become better at your craft is to alter goals to be both more realistic and more specific. You'll also be able to adjust your mindset and approach to your work to improve your output. To that end, there are three "mindsets" as part of the nine keys I have adopted that help me to align my goals and improve my process.

4. The Growth Mindset

"Adjusting your mindset" means altering your approach to thinking, which in turn will alter the way you work.

Adopting a *Growth Mindset* means that you will approach everything you do with growth in mind. Challenges are opportunities to improve oneself or one's skills. Failures are an opportunity to reflect and revise creative methods.

It's an acceptance that you *can* get better, that you *will* get better, and that as you get better more things will be within your reach. You'll be able to play harder music next year. Your next story will be better than the last. If you make a mistake, it's a one less to make in the future.

5. The Professional Mindset

Having a professional mindset means that you think of yourself as a professional – a person both worthy of respect as well as a person actively working in his field in anticipation of profit.

This means leaving self-identifiers such as "aspiring writer" at the door. If you write, you're a writer. If you perform music, you are a musician. If you paint, you're a painter. Adopt that identity!

The opposite of this is the amateur mindset. Amateurs "jam." Professionals "rehearse." You should approach every opportunity with your goals in mind – will writing this story move me closer to my goals? Will joining this band move me closer to my goals? If the answer is no, you should probably move past it.

Being a professional also means having an output. You shouldn't be afraid to publish your book, sell your art, or perform in public. Do the things that you intend to do as a professional in your field right when you begin.

6. The Farmer Mindset

If you have never been a farmer or worked in agriculture, you may not be familiar with the idea of "no sick days." The reality of ag work is that certain things simply must be done on time: no exceptions. Failing to prune your grapevines on time has the potential to wipe out your profits. Calling in sick to the birth of a calf could net you the loss of two cows.

Adopting the farmer mindset means that you don't give yourself excuses when the crunch is on. You show up to do your work, headaches be damned.

This is extremely important for prolific output as skipping work can be a habit in and of itself. Writing a book in a hundred days is only possible if you actually write a thousand words *every* day, not a thousand words every time you *feel* like writing.

You can't win if you don't show up to the match.

7. Avoid Perfectionism

This is the only pointer on the list that is put in the form of a "do not" rather than a "do," but it is a very important pitfall to avoid, whether you truly are a perfectionist or just use it as an excuse to avoid making public your project.

In the short run, aiming for perfection will prevent you from completing creative projects. In the long run, it will harm your ability to progress in the many ways that you cannot see outside of the cycle of project completion. This is because most of the significant problems with your work, the ones which really separate good art from great art, are not flaws in the details, but rather flaws in the approach.

It's not the typos that stop your book from being great (though you should try to minimize those), it's the way you designed the main character. It's not the stray ink mark on your drawing that makes it forgettable, it's the fact that you chose a boring pose for your subject, or that you chose to make your model seven and a half heads tall rather than eight. Many lessons like this will not be learned until you are willing to actually complete a project and put it out for the world to see.

8. Consume Art

This point is one that writers like myself often do a poor job of; we tend to want to spend every waking minute writing and we put off the act of reading or force it into the margins of time.

We create an ideal of ourselves working non-stop at every opportunity, never taking a day or an hour off to do something enjoyable like read a book, or listen to some new music, or play a video game.

You shouldn't do this. First, you will be missing out on techniques that will be useful to you which are present in the work of others. Second, you will be missing the inspiration which drives you to create art in the first place.

9. Break the Rules

One of the hardest parts of being an artist is maintaining the excitement of creation. Trying to constantly adhere to all guidelines for technique or practice can quickly suck the joy out of the creation process.

Breaking the rules (at least a little) will keep you from getting too bogged down in the daily grind and will ensure that you are always innovating.

Rules do exist for good reasons more often than not, but that doesn't mean you have to always do it the proper way. If the proper way is holding you back, it has to go.

9. Break the Rules

Chapter 1: Align Your Priorities for Creative Output

Life is full of demands. Life is full of obligations. Life is full of temptations. Life is often too full of things that each of us wishes to do, and the time during the day is too short to get it all done. The speed of modern life doesn't help, and it is all too easy to find oneself caught up in the cacophony of urban activity and feel completely drained, emotionally and mentally, every day before you can put a minute into your art.

This is the reality of limited time and unlimited wants. When it comes to figuring out how all of it goes together, I have found that priorities are essential, not just to determine a schedule for yourself, but also to make sure what you are doing in your life is what you *actually want to be doing.*

To that important end, before you can decide anything, you have to decide what your priorities actually *are*, rather than what you *wish* for them to be. This is a matter of self-knowledge, not of willpower. It is coming to grips with who you are, not doing algebra with your time. That comes later.

It is *not* useful to do the thought experiment, "What would I do all day if I didn't have to worry about money?"

The result for most artists is the same: I'd make art! However, it's not that simple. Art is almost never created for its own sake, and even when it is, it's still hard, hard work.

Everything you do in life asks something *from* you; there is no pure, easy joy that doesn't have some amount of investment attached to it. Family is a joyful experience but comes at a cost to your time, energy, focus, and bank account. Body-building occurs only though subjecting yourself to pain – literally. Having money to spend is quite nice, but that comes only after you have done the work to acquire it, which can require not only long hours but years of thankless, unprofitable effort.

And yes, creative productivity is hard, hard work with the satisfaction of completion coming only after you have done the work to achieve it, just as it is with money. Yes, money is not everything and you may do a job for reasons besides money, but you should avoid the tempting fantasy of a job being both maximally profitable and maximally enjoyable in the moment.

You aren't going to love every moment in any business. Accept that and go into any endeavor with your eyes open.

Obligations and Focus

When it comes to ordering your priorities for creative output, or even just life in general, I find it helpful to consider what things are obligatory, or unavoidable if you want to maintain your health, sanity, happiness, and integrity, and what things are more optional, or good to have when it is convenient.

The obligatory things will change in priority according to where you are in life. For most people, they break down broadly into:

1. Money
2. Family
3. Health
4. Creativity and Purposeful activities
5. Leisure and Hobbies

6. Social time
7. Life/household Maintenance

You can't really avoid any of these totally. You must have money to live, at least in the modern environment. You have no option but to take out the trash at some point. Sooner or later ignoring your health will catch up to you and you will end up sick or disabled.

These things are also interrelated. Failing health will impact your leisure time and will also impact your ability to gain money.

However, just because these focus areas are obligatory does *not* mean you can do all of them at maximum capacity. I'm writing this on a laptop at my kitchen table, which is covered with mail I haven't thrown away and condiments I never put back up, while my nine-month-old daughter sleeps and my son plays his allotted time of games for the day. I admit I am not optimizing my household maintenance.

My house is messier than others, but I also write books and put out lots of videos. I sacrifice being excellent at my home upkeep in order to work. Likewise, my wife would rather spend time with me or my children than clean, even if she likes the house cleaner than I do. We still clean the house, just not as much or perhaps as thoroughly as other couples might. I also spend less time at the gym compared to when I was single, opting to run for 30 to 40 minutes a night most nights to save time, and going to the gym when I can get my children into bed early. My truck is also quite dusty – I don't wash it except during summer, and not because of water shortages.

This is the self-knowledge part for my wife and me. For both of us, our family is the number one priority. Everything else comes *after* meeting that obligation. Family is where our focus is, and we are happy to sacrifice a messy house, a little income potential (I stay home during the day and my wife only works four days a week), and some social time in order to give the family the attention it needs. I sacrifice those things as well so I can have the time I need to write and produce video content.

We meet some obligations minimally so that we can meet others maximally.

As the focus intensifies, other things become blurry. Less important things become less visible. Having a dusty car only registers because I'm writing about things I tend to ignore.

Those who attempt to be great at everything are probably just mediocre at everything, and that's the unfortunate truth.

What really matters to you? Is there something on that focus and obligations list that wasn't even on your radar? What feels more like a chore than a focus? These are questions you must ask yourself before you begin budgeting your time and trying to make a schedule of your activities.

In my experience, most distress comes not from being unable to order priorities for effectiveness and efficiency, but from attempting to order priorities in a way that goes strongly against your true personality and your mental and emotional needs. You can force yourself to do something that you dislike for a short period of time, but I don't think it's realistic to try to force things that you naturally dislike into becoming natural priorities. If you hate doing dishes, chances are you will always hate it, even if you are very diligent about performing the chore, and if you don't care about an empty sink having one frequently will not instill that care into you.

You have to know who you are. Are you a person that can't stay away from the gym for more than a day? Are you a person who loves working toward the next triathlon? Great, that means fitness and health are a top priority. Sacrificing your gym time to do something else will probably distress you. You need to accept that creativity is a lower concern and enjoy it for what it is. You must put creativity where it truly belongs in your life and schedule.

On the flip side, if you're somebody who hates physical exercise, forcing that to be a top priority will probably cause you distress, even if you achieve the body you are looking for. More than that, you'll probably be upset at your lack of progress as other things distract you and keep you away from your (unrealistic) fitness goals. That doesn't mean you should ignore fitness, it just means you need to be realistic about what kind of time you are truly willing to devote to it, and what time you really can devote to it and still meet your primary obligations.

Making Time

You cannot complain that your day is missing something that is important to you if you do not specifically make time for that thing.

I'll reinforce this to a greater degree in chapter two, but having a consistent work schedule is critical to project completion. Working in a haphazard fashion – perhaps only when you have "free time" – will not only slow you down, it will make the fleeting time you *do* devote to your passion less efficient.

So, the first step to being a prolific creator is having time to create. How much time you have to create, and when during your day you are going to do your creative work, are things you are going to have to decide for yourself *after* you have figured out where creativity is relative to the other obligations in your life.

What is important when making this decision is treating creative work as true work – as an *obligation*. You should view your work as something you *must* do, ideally every single day, before your day is complete.

Just as an example, consider this schedule:

6:30 AM – wake up, get coffee, etc.
7:30 AM – Leave for work
8:00 AM – Arrive at work
5:00 PM – Leave work
5:30 PM – Gym time
6:30 PM – Head Home
7:00 PM – Arrive home, have dinner
8:00 PM – Watch TV
9:00 PM – Get the kids to bed
10:00 PM – Go to bed.

This schedule is very simple and missing lots of things, but it represents is a typical sort of day for most people. They might have extra things in there, like taking the children to soccer practice, but it's very standard.

A person with this schedule might conclude that they should do creative work on the weekends or cut out TV time and make that hour a creative block. It's a good start, but you will probably need *some* leisure time if you don't want to go crazy.

When I had a schedule like this (when I taught full time), I spent more than three hours per day being creative, and I was more productive than an average person in those three hours.

I'll give some strategies to that effect later on, in Chapter 2, but it all comes down to priorities.

Now, let's take a look at those seven obligations and see how they relate to our primary goal – being creative.

1. Money

Personal finances, for most people, are something that can only be ignored at perilous risk. We live in a world where we cannot provide for all of our needs, so we must earn money to pay for most of what we consume. Even a stay-at-home parent must carefully manage a budget to ensure the needs of the family are met, even if the duty of earning the income is assigned to the other parent.

Money, however, is not something that has to be the primary focus for all people. Those who really focus on making money, investing, or creating businesses can tell you just how much hard work goes into getting rich. A lot has to be sidelined if you are going to be spending twelve hours per day building up your business for a secure tomorrow.

It's not just the time spent at the job, but also the mental focus. Make no mistake, business is its own creative endeavor and will occupy "headspace," for lack of a better term.

My wife often remarks on how she knows I'm disconnected from the moment, thinking of something related to my businesses – new book ideas, new video ideas, something with marketing, etc. My biggest periods of dissonance actually came not from being out of the moment, but from having these "out of time" moments be occupied by work thoughts which I didn't actually care about, like when my day job was as a public school teacher and I had a million problems to solve every week. Teaching took up a great amount of head-space I wanted free for other things.

If working 60 hours a week at a job or business isn't for you, you aren't alone, which is why most people pick a job that gives maximum payout for minimum work, rather than pursuing the bottom line with relentless fervor. There's nothing wrong with going to work for eight hours (or less), clocking out, and then going home. There's nothing wrong with having a roomy budget that doesn't put the maximum amount into savings every month.

All this just means that finances aren't your area of personal excellence and aren't a huge priority. That also means your time and, more importantly, your mental energy, is freed up for other pursuits.

Let me also say that many, many people in the creative fields I interact with (primarily writing, music, and visual arts) have early illusions that they can combine the obligation of money with their creative output – in effect, they can make a great living while doing what they love.

This is a myth, unfortunately, but not because it isn't possible to make money as a creative professional, but rather because any business venture will ask you to do things that you don't readily enjoy. Authors must also be marketers. Musicians must also be booking agents and producers. It won't be pure joyful work when you are actually doing it for a living.

In addition, most people new to their field believe they will be immediately successful and be able to quit their day job right away. The truth is that most immediate success is a fluke. If you actually want to find success it will take a lot of investment of time, if not money, before you start to see returns. Most businesses lose money early on, and your creative business will probably not be an exception.

This brings me back to money – having enough is important, but you need to leave room in your schedule and your head if you want to make creative gains as well. Consider how much time you really want to work before getting to your real work – creating art.

You should consider this before taking a job – the bottom line might be nice, but does it leave room for your creative work in both your schedule and your head?

Going back to that example schedule – what if you left work at three PM? What if you only worked four days per week? How much more room would you have in your life to pack your day with what really matters? Consider this when deciding how to arrange your life.

2. Family

One of the most prolific composers of the Baroque period, Johann Sebastian Bach, had a total of 24 children across two marriages while being the music director at five churches at once. He usually wrote a new cantata (a fairly large and complex composition) every week.

I bring this up because our society is full of messages that a fulfilling career and family are at odds with one another, when they aren't. I've known musicians who tour extensively, all over the world, and who still have families. Active military personnel, who are often deployed for long stretches of time, still have families.

If your own family is something you really want in your life, you can have it, *and* you can still have a creative career, but like with anything, understanding focus priorities is key.

Family is, by necessity, a lower priority for those who have to spend large amounts of time away from family, such as touring musicians or men engaged in active military service. This doesn't mean that they *care* less about their family, since what they are doing is often done specifically to provide *for* a family; I'm merely saying that, in terms of time and focus, family is lower on the list than professional obligations. The same goes for businessmen who spend long hours working or traveling.

People are often dishonest with themselves when it comes to preferences, though, and if you aren't a homebody you shouldn't feel bad about wanting to pour more of your time into your creative projects or your work. Ideally, if you are married and having children, you have a partner with a complementary set of preferences that prefers more time with the kids or is at least willing to give you time to be creative.

When it comes to family, negotiating the balance between obligations is more complicated, because you aren't the only party.

If you are somebody who doesn't prefer to have his or her own family, family itself is probably still somewhere on the obligation list, even if it is just siblings and parents over the holidays.

Family (to me, anyway) also includes your primary romantic relationship, as that has the trajectory to become a family, even if you don't have children. Just like any life area you develop, time with your romantic partner is a kind of investment. The return is a strong relationship that can sustain periods of separation that are both brief (like gigging on Saturday nights) and prolonged (like going on tour).

If you want to make progress on your goals, you need to be spending time on them. Labels like "mom" and "dad" need not be your entire identity – in fact, I think it is good for my children to see and understand the work their parents do, as this helps them to understand just who their parents *are.*

For me, most of my time is spent on family. Most of my work happens in the margins, but that is how I prefer it. My children are (as I am writing this) still very young and dependent. I will only have that time with them once; I cannot go back in time if I miss portions of their young childhood. When they get older, I know their need for me will diminish and they will become more independent, so my priorities can (and probably will) change in a few years' time.

It's a bit hard for me to step away from my kids to work (while they are awake), but sometimes I need to do that to meet my creative and business goals.

3. Health and Fitness

Health, like finance, needs to be a priority on some level for every single person. Ignoring your health will have a massively negative impact on you *and* your creative output.

First, you will be unable to do your work with maximum efficiency and effectiveness. If you are tired from lack of sleep, your focus will be shot, and you won't be able to write. If you ignore a problem like diabetes, you won't be able to function mentally, and you may lose time to being physically ill. Likewise, if your weight is out of control, you will lack the physical capacity to perform live as a musician.

Second, ignoring your health will shorten your life. That smoking habit *will* take its toll, eventually. Obesity will catch up with you at some point and you'll have heart problems that can't be easily fixed by the medical establishment. You'll also go from health that allows you to work to being disabled earlier in your life. All of that will shrink the amount of creative work you can do over the long term.

On the other hand, you can sacrifice your health to increase your output in the short term. Artists of varying kinds have taken amphetamines and other stimulants to avoid sleep and work relentlessly, but such a lifestyle comes at a large cost, especially as time goes on.

For some people, fitness and health is their absolute top priority, and that's fine too if that is you. Exercise will help you live longer and enjoy the life you have to a greater extent, but there is always a cost, usually in the form of time, but it could also be risk of injury and wear and tear on your body.

The main thing is, to keep your creative output consistent, you need to pay attention to your health in some capacity. Working optimally for an hour because you are well-rested is probably better than working two hours while fighting sleep or being sick. Not all time spent is equally productive, something I hope I will continue to convince you of throughout this book.

I'll address this later, but lots of people give themselves too much slack when they have a cold. If you are truly ill (for me that means throwing up or in horrific pain) it is fine to rest, but having a cold doesn't mean you should be totally out of commission, especially when you have a deadline to meet. Getting that little bit of work done at what capacity you have will be important over the long-term.

4. Creativity and Purposeful Activities

Here is where we get to producing art. A creative endeavor is something you do because you have a need to create something, to put something out into the world. Painting, music, writing, or even something like winemaking, are realms of passion, not merely realms of economic activity. Creativity is always something more than a job.

Purposeful activities are fundamentally different from creative endeavors, though they fulfill some of the same. These are things like charity or volunteer work, which are intended to make a difference in the lives of others but aren't done because there is an internal need for those things to exist on their own. Likewise, though they may provide economic benefit, they are not something that is done for the purposes of income.

Art is you facing the world, charity is you loving the world.

If you are reading this, passions are probably already a high priority, or you at least you desire for them to be a higher priority. Lots, if not most, artists wish they had more time to work.

If this is you, what you first must recognize is that creativity is an obligation, not just an activity to fit into the margins or something to be done only when you feel like it. Just like how you exercise regularly to stay physically healthy, you must also exercise your creative mind to stay spiritually healthy.

Putting creativity in the same place as everything else will ensure it becomes a permanent and habitual part of your life. Additionally, if you want to understand the real secret to being prolific, it is consistent work. Doing it daily has always been the best course for every student I have had, and I can usually tell when they have stuck to a practice schedule (speaking mostly of music here). Within a very short time their growth skyrockets. Over time the leaps are gargantuan. Or, if they haven't stuck to it, we have the same lesson several weeks in a row.

I exercise every day. I also write every day. There are a few exceptions, but these are reasonable, like extreme ill-health or travel. Just writing one thousand words per day will potentially yield three (or even four) full-length novels per year. Impressive!

If you can't do something creative every day (and there may be good reasons for this – if you have odd work shifts or longer than normal days a few times a week), try to at least be consistent week-to-week. I record most of my YouTube videos on Saturday, and I always have a live stream on Wednesday. That lets me keep my daily work focused on my writing or (if I am in that place) my music.

A note on sub-categories

Just like how you can't be great at every large area of priority in your life, you can't be good at all the things which fit into each category. I'm a writer, video content maker, and musician. I can't be equally good at all of those, so I prioritize writing and other things are forced more into the margins. Some seasons, I switch that and focus entirely on music or on producing content. Generally, the more focused you are on one thing, the more efficient you become with your work time.

5. Leisure and Hobbies

I think for most people who are imagining themselves as productive machines, their idealized self isn't actively engaging in lots of leisure. Again, though, self-knowledge is key. Some people spend far too much time on video games, but plenty of others work hard so they can enjoy an hour or two of gaming a day.

If I totally avoid leisure activities I suffer mentally and emotionally. I need a certain amount of downtime to flourish, and If I don't get it, I find it is very difficult for me to be happy creating.

At the same time, I also think the consumption of art, which can include leisure activities like reading, is fundamental to keeping the creative well filled.

So, don't make the mistake of trying to schedule out all fun from your day in hopes you will be more productive. Chances are you won't make as much progress as you wish and you will get burned out that much faster.

Some people also have serious hobbies that occupy a central role in their lives. These can be something like playing Dungeons or Dragons, or golfing. To me, a hobby is different than a purposeful activity, because a hobby is done for personal enjoyment, whereas the creation of art is done for both intrinsic and extrinsic reasons related to completion and transmission of a product.

Nevertheless, some people take their Warhammer, or their Magic the Gathering, or their golf game very seriously.

My general caution regarding hobbies of this sort is that they tend to act as a proxy for life output, and thus make you feel like you are being productive when you are really just engaging in leisure.

It feels good to get Gladiator or Grand Marshall in World of Warcraft, but did the time spent reaching that pinnacle truly net you anything real and lasting? I could honestly say the same about your golf game, but we are trained to think of things like golf as being fundamentally different than video games, when the two activities, if judged by outputs, aren't much different.

In my opinion and experience, hobbies are something that should be put in significant check if you want to be making gains in your creative output. You can have one, but more than that is going suck up your time (and possibly your paycheck) in a big way.

Choose wisely what you do in your downtime, because putting limitations on leisure is one of the most important things you can do to make sure your output is consistent. Make time for your games – the amount of time you need to relax and enjoy the activity, but *only* spend the time you *have budgeted.*

Leisure is also one of the things that you have to let go of in a pinch, so be ready to let it go when a deadline looms.

6. Social Time

We are social beings. We live in groups. Social time is important. Our social nature is also something that is exploited by social media to suck our time and attention away from other matters, and this is something you *must* be aware of.

Depending on your stage of life and personal attitude, social time is something that can be either minimal or all-consuming. It's also an area of life that few people are honest about when it comes to acknowledging their preferences.

Very few individuals actually fit the "lone wolf" archetype. Even fewer can spend ten hours a day writing by themselves.

Some people are by nature extremely social, preferring a large quantity of time spent on social interaction. In my experience, young people are more social than older people, and probably for good reason, since a well-established friendship or marriage from youth will provide support throughout life.

I find that having a limited budget of social time (as we used to think of it) is not such a difficult thing now, but it once was, and potentially still could be for some people. When I was a music student, I wasted copious amounts of time socializing. It was very easy to do this, as the music department at my university was full of tables, benches, foyers, and other gathering spaces, and these gathering spaces were all full of other artists.

That was great for comradeship, and even building professional relationships relating to performance, but it was very bad for productivity. Once I figured out that too much social time was a time sink and spent some effort developing some self-discipline and setting a schedule, my productivity skyrocketed. I didn't really have it all figured out until I was more than two years into the program and there is a marked difference between my work those first two years and the work I did my second two years.

I became a truly prolific composer and performer during that period (and I also wrote my first attempt at a novel, which was awful, but more on that later). I gigged every week with a band, learned hours of solo repertoire which I performed regularly, and composed hours and hours of music.

It really was my social time holding me back, but I never abandoned social time. I just held it in check to mealtimes, between closely scheduled classes, and parties. Any chunk of time more than ten minutes in duration I spent practicing or working on new music.

It was great at the time, but I don't think I would have done as well these days. Social media has changed everything.

Social Media

Social media has drastically changed the way we approach social interaction.

When I was young, we had to call each other on the phone or otherwise be physically present with one another to communicate. Even text messaging was new and (mostly) annoying when I was in college and the smartest phone was a flip phone.

Now, calls are a rarity and social media substitutes for a great degree of social interaction. Sites like Facebook are designed to hijack the social reward centers of our brains and feed us small dopamine rushes throughout the day, turning interacting with the site into a habit, or in some cases, an addiction.

It's possible to waste *huge* amounts of time on social media every day, and I think most people are largely unaware of it. If you took a day to legitimately track the time spent on social media, you might be shocked to see how much time you have wasted. I know Android devices can track screen time. Try looking up yours sometime.

If you are jumping at the chance to reclaim a few hours a day for creative work, slow down. The thing is, a lot of that time is spread out into little bite-sized chucks - time that would likely be lost in the flow of the day anyway. However, social media's omnipresence also means that it occupies headspace and is a constant distraction.

While you are checking Facebook, you aren't thinking of your project. That's time lost.

It also can affect your mindset - *what if nobody liked your post? Why is everyone else successful besides you? CNN SAYS THE WORLD IS ENDING.* Facebook's filtering mechanisms ensure that you see things which engage you (most often fear-mongering news or hot-takes, since fear and anger are the most immediate emotions) and the userbase only posts positive highlights like fancy dinners and beach trips - leading you to believe that your life is worse by comparison.

The problem is, the contemporary artist *needs* to be on social media. It's the best and cheapest method of attracting an audience and building professional relationships in your field. As a creative, you cannot pull the plug without significantly harming your business.

So what to do?

Here are my suggestions. You can do all or some of these:

1. **Set a time for actual social media interaction.** Do not exceed the allotted time! I usually answer YouTube comments only at one or two times per day, for a limited number of minutes. This ensures that I still interact with my channel and that I also focus only on responding to comments that really are worth responding to. Good times for social media time would be when waking up and after getting home, or when using the bathroom.

2. **If you feel bored, read instead of looking at social media.** EBooks are very cheap, and blogs are free.

You can be learning or reading a great story instead of flipping through photos of people you don't talk to anymore.

3. **Turn off all notifications on your phone.** This will ensure that you are not distracted and, if you are going to look at social media, it is because you at least have some time for it.

4. **Develop a specific social media strategy for your business.** This will focus your interaction toward customers and other professionals. Are you posting about music? Are you talking about books? Are you passing out hot takes to get attention and using the follow-up to promote yourself?

5. **Spend time with real people.** For me, a great part of my social time each day is virtual, and this is how it has to be. My social time with real people is limited because of my intense schedule, but I do my best to at least have lunch with a friend every once in a while.

I almost never look at Facebook now. I'm on twitter all the time. I'm on YouTube the most, as that is where most of my audience is. You have to find where you are going to get the best exposure for your art and your personality type.

7. Maintenance

What I classify as "maintenance" are all the little obligations you have as part of living: cleaning the house, taking out the trash, fixing faucets, fixing cars, mowing the lawn, etc.

I also include feeding yourself and performing basic hygiene.

This is one area where I see an intense amount of focus directed toward things like "life hacks" – little things that either save time or improve your effectiveness at life maintenance in the long run. I saw an ad for a device called the "Y Toothbrush" that claimed it could clean your teeth in ten seconds. I just watched a two-minute video on it, which is how much time I could have spent just brushing my teeth. But it's tempting to consider it since over the course of a year I would save 24 hours of time. Wow!

The thing is, I think most of these things are of only marginal usefulness as far as saving time goes. 24 hours sounds like a lot, but when it is in two-minute intervals you could easily lose all of that time looking at twitter and not gain anything for your investment.

Meal prepping is a great example of this focus on making the mundane efficient. Lots of people swear by it – you spend part of Sunday prepping all of your meals for the coming week, then you just pop them in the oven (or microwave) during the weekday rush. You aren't saving time – you are shifting time from a day where you feel busy to one where you don't feel busy. This can be a big gain – *if* you use the time saved each day productively.

That's not what I do, though. I eat roughly the same three meals a day, every day. No headspace taken up thinking about food, it's easy to manage the diet and macros, and all of the meals I can make in five minutes anyway. Diet variety is something I don't care about.

I don't care about meals very much because I *really* care about the other things I want to do, like writing and playing with my children. I put maintenance in the margins, rather than my creativity.

Paper plates, plastic spoons, and Styrofoam cups.

Let me share an anecdote with you. Some of you will hate me for this, but that's okay if you get the lesson.

When I lived in Las Vegas, my roommate Matt (who would eventually become my brother-in-law) and I had a problem. We hated doing dishes and we also kept plugging up the dishwasher with whey protein and dried milk (we were both big into fitness at the time). It was getting annoying, and we came up with a solution.

We spent the next two years eating on nothing but paper plates and drinking from nothing besides Styrofoam cups (or soda cans). We cooked almost all of our meals on a twenty-dollar George Foreman electric grill. We ate the same few meals every day.

We figured out we could buy the plates, cups, and spoons (which we used exclusively for protein shakes) cheaply from Costco (we bought Styrofoam because it was cheaper than paper), we no longer had to spend any time on dishes (which was something we hated doing anyway), we no longer had to buy soap for the dishes, and there was no conflict whatsoever in managing domestic maintenance as a result, as the kitchen was 50% of the shared space, with the other half being the washer and dryer.

It cost us about 15 extra dollars a month, split two ways. We could take a drink to the gym (or anywhere else) and just toss it. We had to empty the trash more often, which was not a big deal compared to the alternative – doing dishes.

This was legitimately the only life hack that ever worked for me, and it was one that just happened to fit my situation.

Maintenance as a priority.

Where you put household maintenance is largely a part of what you need as a person. If you need to have a very clean house, you have to find ways to do that as efficiently and effectively as possible.

For me, a perfect house is not a need. Dusty shelves don't bug me except every so often; same with dirty mirrors. Eventually, they do bother me, but cleaning the mirrors once every other month is less time and effort than cleaning them every week. That's just reality.

Whatever your needs, you do have to accept the fact that having a perfect house will take time (and headspace) away from other activities. What will you give up if this is something you must have?

Personal maintenance

I think if there is one sub-area where you should *not* try to cut corners, it is personal hygiene and beauty. This is especially the case if you are a woman. Speaking completely honestly, women are judged much more harshly for their looks than men are, and this includes judgment by other women. For a woman, skipping makeup is not an option and personal dress is both more complicated and more important.

You want to look your best if you are a performer or anyone who shows his or her face on social media. Looks matter. As an artist, you are marketing yourself, not just your art. Having your beard trimmed or face shaved will make you look better and people will like you better for it. Having your hair neatly arranged and wearing clothes that fit properly will make people pay better attention to you.

I've learned this through experience. Last year I hacked my beard down and suddenly everyone thought I had lost a bunch of weight. It was an immediate aesthetic upgrade, and people noticed. In fact, comments on my appearance, particularly my hair, are very common on my YouTube channel.

People notice your appearance.

Working in the Margins

Let's look at that schedule from before:

6:30 AM – wake up, get coffee, etc.

7:30 AM – Leave for work

8:00 AM – Arrive at work

5:00 PM – Leave work

5:30 PM – Gym time

6:30 PM – Head Home

7:00 PM – Arrive home, have dinner

8:00 PM – Watch TV

9:00 PM – Get the kids to bed

10:00 PM – Go to bed.

I think this is the way most people think of scheduling. I had a very similar schedule when I was a high school teacher. In reality, it is not as tight a schedule as it looks, because things are missing from it. Let me tell you how my schedule actually panned out:

6:30 AM – Wake up

7:00 AM – Out the door, get coffee/Rockstar on the way to work.

7:15-7:55 – I record a podcast with my brother-in-law (also an author and musician) on our commute to work

8 AM – Begin work

9:45 AM – Union-mandated fifteen-minute break. Master audio recording and upload the podcast, check social media.

11:40 AM – Union mandated 45 minute lunch begins. Eat for five minutes while prepping to write. Write for 40 minutes.

12:25 PM – Union-negotiated prep period. I perform whatever work-related tasks are appropriate, then write the rest of the hour.

3:00 PM – School ends. According to union negotiations, I have to stay in my room another hour. I write.

4:00 PM – If I have no performances at night, head home. Relax, listen to music, and talk shop with my brother-in-law on the way.

5 PM – Gym time.

6 PM – Get home. Dinner Time / Family time

8 PM – Additional work time, as much as I need to get done that day

9 PM – read to my son, he goes to sleep.

10 PM onward – more work time or sleep.

Looking back, this was a very loose and easy schedule for me to keep, and I got to work a lot. In fact, I got to work much more than I do now. Having only one child helped, as did the fact that my wife stayed home and did most of the home maintenance while I was away.

You might notice that I cut time in some places. I showered after the gym, not in the morning. I had a longer commute than most, and I turned it into productive time to market my books. I viewed lunch as free time to work, not relax or socialize, instead getting my relaxing and socializing done on my commute home. I viewed 8 hours of sleep as optional, and I often took the option to stay up and finish important tasks.

I got a lot of work done in the margins – the little spaces between other things that go wasted by most people. However, I *always* still had time specifically set aside for working on my creative goals. At the very bare minimum, you *must* schedule time to work, or you will find it simply is not there.

Chapter 2: Establish a Creative Process

The process for creation must come before the goals.

This seems unintuitive until you have been working in the field for some time. After all, most people get into a creative field with some sort of goal in mind – writing a book, recording an album, or something more general like "being a painter."

There is absolutely nothing wrong with having goals, but you have to ask yourself, "How am I going to get there? What am I going to do *once I do* get there?" Having a goal is ultimately meaningless without a method by which you will accomplish it. More than that, a good process will keep you working toward even more goals – not just your first book, but your fifth, or tenth, and will also inform you as to what goals are even possible.

Your process and your goals should align. The chief way in which you will evaluate the efficacy of your process is by judging how well it moves you forward toward your goals. A process that doesn't deliver sufficient outputs, or delivers outputs other than those which are desired, must be revised.

However, if you are starting out, it can be very difficult to know exactly how to establish a process. I've come up with a few guidelines that I think work across all creative fields but bear in mind that different fields have different outputs and different people have different strengths and weaknesses, which will alter how they approach their craft. My specialties, writing and music, will receive some detailed suggestions. For those operating in other fields (such as visual arts) a great way to start establishing a process is to ask professionals in your field as to how they approach work.

Here are my general guidelines for any creative process:

1) Make it part of your daily routine
2) Have a goal for each work session
3) Have a routine that structures your work time
4) Create a macro process that involves starting and completing new projects
5) Make the world aware of your work.

From this you might have ascertained that a creative process exists on three levels:

1) What you do while you are working
2) What you do day to day and week to week
3) What you do season to season or project to project

In other words, you will need a process that is repeatable every time you sit down to work, a place for that process in your schedule every day, and an understanding of how your process needs to change or reset as you move through the stages on project completion. I'll give some specifics for each one of these; figuring out how to have a repeatable process at the macro, or project level, is generally the most advanced thing you will need to learn.

Daily Routine

Going back to the concept of priorities, I said that creative work needs to be an obligation, similar to everything else in your life if you want to be making progress towards the completion of a project. For some people who must work schedules that make a daily routine impossible, try to make at least a weekly routine that includes regular work. If you work totally irregular hours, try to make it an obligation, like doing laundry, that you do when you finally have free time.

I recommend an hour or more. Usually, it takes me at least a few minutes to disengage from the other distractions of life and get in the zone to write. If you are trying to work in 15-minute increments (which I often do at times by necessity), you might be losing a lot of time in transition. But even if you only have 15 minutes, it is still better than nothing.

So, pick a time and make it yours. Turn off the phone, close out any social media distractions, and work for the time you have given yourself. It should be a time when you are truly able, mentally and physically, to attend to the task at hand.

For me, I write primarily late at night, after my family has gone to sleep. Once I get the kids in bed I exercise, and then I have my writing time. This works well for me because the ending time is open to change as needed, and the start time can vary depending on how my children are. Sometimes they get to sleep earlier, sometimes later. I always have *my time*, though. I try to always work at least an hour. If I am approaching a deadline, I know that I can stay up to get things done.

I've had friends who do the opposite. They set an alarm before the children wake up and work a set time until they leave for work or have to attend to the family. This works better for some people who suffer mental fatigue as the day goes on. For me, I'm sharper at night. Do what works for you and don't be afraid to try out something different.

I also end my day with things that aren't work, like a game or book (or occasionally a TV show or a piece of a movie – I don't usually like TV shows). This is a "cool down" for me so that my mind can stop attending to constant thoughts about my current project and allow me to get some sleep.

In general, the more consistently and frequently you are engaging in your work, the faster you will complete a project. Each minute spent is one minute closer to the finished product. There is a compound benefit to this regimented approach as well – the more you work, the better you get at working.

Working consistently will make your work more effective. When you first start writing, you might be lucky to write 500 words in an hour. After a few weeks, you'll be writing 1,000 words in an hour, effectively doubling your output without changing anything else. This works as well with music. The more you practice, the more effective each session gets, which means you learn music more quickly, which in turn means your progress accelerates. There are limits to this, but if you haven't been working consistently before, you can expect to see extreme growth once you get this down.

Getting work time in your schedule is the first and most critical step. In fact, if you just start working without any concrete goal you will still see a benefit in the form of growth, along with an ability to set your goals more realistically as you better understand your abilities and working speed (more on that later).

I'll also write in a bit about alternatives to the daily routine, for those of you for whom that just isn't going to work.

Setting Up Your Work Environment

The environment you choose to work in can have a large effect on your productivity, usually in the way that it affects your focus and stamina.

A workplace that offers up constant interruptions from others will impact your workflow, just as setting up shop among temptations can negatively affect focus. Ideally, both your time and your space will be dedicated, at least in the time that you have scheduled for your work, toward your creative work.

For me, this means that during my set-aside work time my office door is closed and my children are not allowed to interrupt me. It's not perfect, as I can often hear them playing down the hallway, but it is much better than attempting to work on the kitchen table or with a laptop in the living room. Often my wife will take the opportunity to take the kids out of the house – either to something like the park or to visit a relative if it is on the weekend.

I also silence my phone and make a point to avoid social media and other distractions while I work. I know that if I want my time to be fully productive, having my mind totally on what I am doing is key.

Having a set time and special space makes transitioning to a work-focused mind much easier. When you enter that space, you know you are there to work. It's similar to ideas of sleep hygiene, in which you eliminate from your bedroom activities which are not related to sleep, such as TV, busywork, or reading.

To that end, one of the things I started doing a few years ago was choosing to play my video games on a console rather than on my PC. While the graphics are superior on my computer, moving that activity to another room made it much easier for me to get into the correct headspace for creative work. Now when I fire up my computer, my thoughts immediately go to the day's work, not a recent game.

This isn't possible with every game type. MMORPGs (massively multiplayer online roleplaying games, such as World of Warcraft) don't function well on console, and FPS games are, compared to using a keyboard and a mouse, unplayable using a controller. I've ended up mostly abandoning these playstyles as time has gone on, just as an unintended consequence of this approach. I lament it slightly because I loved playing MMOs, but ultimately work comes first.

Not everyone has the option of an office or studio, either because they lack the extra space in their home or can't justify the expense of renting one. For these people, my best advice is to pick a space that is only minimally used for other activities, such as the kitchen table rather than the living room or bedroom. Make sure that during your specified work time there are none of those other activities going on. If you are working on the kitchen table, get to work after everyone has moved onto other things in other rooms.

This is why most bands start out as garage bands – the garage is a space big enough to hold a band and also has minimal alternative use. Simply move the car out, and you have a rehearsal space, at least for the night. Lots of writers in the past had "writing sheds" which usually amounted to a tool shed with a typewriter, which works as well. When rehearsing with your band, you won't be distracted by wanting to work on your car, just as you won't be distracted by wanting to do your gardening when sitting in your shed.

I should also mention there are writers who do something which for a long time made no sense to me: writing at Starbucks. I've worked in a variety of sub-optimal environments due to the necessities of life, but these aren't usually something I would *choose*. Starbucks *could* be a good choice for a writer, despite its general noisiness and crowds, because it is a space apart from the home where the mind can stop focusing on domestic burdens. The noise is, at some point, more like white noise: something that becomes unnoticed and drowns out detailed, distracting noises.

There is also the *benefit* of distraction at Starbucks.

This may sound counter-intuitive but having small opportunities for selected distractions can actually help workflow. Shifting your focus for a few moments can give you a release of the tension of work, making the moments you focus more enjoyable and productive. Don't forget that focus is like a muscle, and you aren't going to be extremely strong with your focus early into your career when you haven't spent any time "flexing" it.

This selected distraction could be something as simple as a window to look out of while you work, or it could be a cat that likes to sit on the top of your chair. The important thing is that the distraction is not long-lasting or of substantial relative interest. Watching people talk in Starbucks, or watching people walk by on occasion, is this sort of distraction. More interesting things, like watching TV, are not advisable unless you are doing something that requires so little of your focus you can do with not attending to the task very much, like running on a treadmill.

At one point, I watched television while practicing guitar. This allowed me to focus for only a few minutes at a time when it was hard to do so. It also allowed me to get through some very brutal repetitions without getting bored to tears. I learned classical guitar tremolo in just a few days this way, repeating the pattern over and over while watching the nightly hour of the Simpsons. Tremolo is a very specific pattern (thumb, then ring, middle, and index fingers on a single string) that must be played at high speed. High repetition with little focus was acceptable for this activity.

It would not be acceptable for something that required lots of thought, such as music composition.

Practice Zombies - Have a goal for each session

Don't go into the practice room without an idea of what you want to do there.

Let me explain from the perspective of music:

If you have ever been involved in music in school, you might have had your instructor tell you to "practice," and complain that the band or choir isn't practicing enough. Rarely does an instructor tell you what you ought to do when practicing, or more importantly, what you should expect to get done during a session.

Most music departments at the university level are haunted by what I call "practice zombies." These are students who know they need to spend time practicing (two hours or some other large chunk of time their instructor says they must), so they drift into a practice room when they have nothing else to do, pull out their instrument, and do what amounts to nothing for a while.

It may look like they are practicing, but they aren't. They are usually doing a few things:

1. Playing scales
2. Doing long tones (even funnier if they play clarinet or saxophone)
3. Working through etudes
4. Playing pieces that they already know

5. Staring into space
6. Chatting with other students who walked by

Perhaps you have seen some of these students in the wild. They need not be students, either. I knew a fellow who used to stop by the practice rooms every day because he knew he needed it in his routine; another friend of mine said about him, "I see him in there every day, but he never gets any better!"

Practice zombies are focusing on doing things that are easy, rather than things that are hard - things which will move them forward and create growth. You should sound *bad* in the practice room because you should be focusing on things that you *can't do yet*. Practice zombification was compounded in students who practiced outside. If people are listening, you are going to turn your session into a performance, focusing on what you can already do to avoid embarrassment.

What they should be doing is setting goals for their session. Example:

1. Play measures 32-40 100% cleanly at 80% tempo or faster.
2. Play measure 52 cleanly at 100% tempo
3. Play the A section by memory
4. Play through my newest repertoire with the time remaining

This approach to practice ensures there is always *not* enough practice time, but this realistic – there is never quite enough time. Spending your time with this order of priorities (remember the importance of ordering priorities? It's important for work time, too) ensures that whatever time you do spend practicing is always moving you forward by the maximum amount. You are always doing whatever is the highest priority, usually the most difficult part or a piece you will be performing soon, and saving unimportant things for when you have accomplished your primary goal. Notice that run-throughs are saved for the end, not the beginning. Your run-though, ideally, would inform what you need to work on for the next day or week.

While this approach to work time cannot readily be transferred outside of music performance, the approach certainly can be. Always ask yourself:

1. What needs my attention *now?*
2. What needs my attention *today?*
3. What needs my attention *at some point.*

Then you structure your work to reflect those needs. For me, there is often something that has to be done immediately. Usually, it is a task I prefer not to address, like fixing something on my website or making sure my content is visible and active. That may seem the opposite of what a prolific writer should be doing (like working on books), but it is imperative that I keep my marketing machine going if I want to sell books. That means I need to make frequent (ideally daily) content.

After that, I work on my daily goal. I always write a thousand words minimum on my current book, more if I can or if I feel I'm in the zone (or much less if I am in the editing phase of a book; that's part of the macro process). A thousand words, in truth, is not very much but it adds up big time over the long term.

Then if I still have time I work on other long-term stuff – setting up and optimizing emails, ads, and social media profiles, etc.

For Writers

For writers, I recommend you set a daily word count goal. If you are new to the discipline, start at 500 words (about one single-spaced page in Times New Roman 12-point font). If that doesn't take up your entire budgeted time, try 1,000 words. Then 1,500.

For reference, Stephen King wrote 2,500 words per day in his prime, and he is massively prolific. As a "retiree" he writes 1,500. This is a perfect example of how having a daily routine and a daily goal can net huge returns over time.

Some pulp authors claim that they can push 10,000 words in a day. I've done this before, but it is unrealistic for most people who won't be able to focus that intently for such a long time day after day. We'll talk more about sprints, where you do large amounts of work in a short time, later on. The point I want to get across here is that you should set a modest goal in terms of word count and stick to it. Consistency with each session is more important than having a big day.

Also, you should never edit while you are writing a draft. That will turn you into the literary version of a practice zombie.

For Artists

Visual arts, such as painting or graphic novels, are a different beast. It's good to set a goal for what you are doing, but sometimes those goals are a bit difficult to define. How does one define "progress" on a detailed painting?

I've discovered that the most consistent artists usually have some way of defining progress. They will break a painting down into its parts and have a goal for each part. For instance, on day 1, they will sketch the planned painting. On day

2, they will perform a basic color study of the piece, changing what details they need. On day 3, they will begin the final piece, usually starting with the subject or a portion of the subject - for instance, the entirety of the figure minus details. Then they add in each part – the face, the background, the clothing details, and final touches, in order to complete a piece.

You'll have to find a way of breaking things down in this way, depending on the type of art you are producing.

For comic artists and graphic novel artists, goals might be easier to set. First, you have to have a basic story sketch of your planned book (with dialogue hopefully already written), then you work on pencils, then inking. From there, you can decide what you should get done each day – say one page fully inked once you are working on the final project. The greats used to put out large volumes simply because they were on a timeline for release and designed their art to match the necessity of a release schedule. This might mean using baroque detail only on large panels or full-page splashes and cutting out the background on most passing panels.

Having a similar approach will help you to decide what panels need high detail and which ones can have a simpler approach without disrupting the flow of the story.

For Music Composers

Music composition, to me, is just as nebulous as art as far as tracking "progress" and making small goals goes, as each composer has a different approach to constructing their music. Some people start with a melody, then add accompaniment, others (like me) write almost everything all at once.

Defining a goal is still important, though. If I am composing, I try to complete one section (usually 16-64 measures, depending on the piece) per day or more, so I can finish a piece in a weekend. Then, once finished, I edit the music and put on all the final details. If I am creating a score, I leave out all articulations and other directions until the end, as trying to write all of that in, especially in a score writing program, is very cumbersome and takes me out of the flow of composition.

Work Routines

Besides actually making time to work, it is a good idea to have a specific routine for your work time itself. This will ensure that you get into your creative headspace quickly and reliably and that you are able to disengage from the project when you need to. Here is a good example from the music field that I used to suggest to my students:

1. Warm-up (5 minutes)
2. Etudes (10 minutes)
3. New Music (30 minutes)
4. Run-throughs (10-15 minutes)
5. Notes for the next day

You can see with this routine, that you have something that gets you into the space to play, something which helps growth (the etudes – or pieces of music designed to test technique), and then you are immediately doing work on something new, reserving run-throughs of any complete pieces for the end. This fits the priorities I mentioned earlier and will prevent the student from entering the realm of the "practice zombie." Writing down what to work on the next day releases your mind and lets you focus on your next task.

It could also be easily expanded to take up more than an hour, or less, by expanding or shrinking everything. When I was actively performing, I spent almost no time on run-throughs of established material, since I performed that repertoire live several times per week.

For writing, I do something different:

1. Read the previous day's work (correct things if needed)
2. Pre-write – think about what I'm writing and maybe write down a sentence of what is going to happen.
3. Write until the word-count goal is met
4. Read or play a game

Playing a game might seem unrelated, but it serves the same point as reading a book – not enhancing my craft but rather getting my mind off of the work so I can sleep (I write at night). When I skip that transition, I often have trouble sleeping and lose the time I would spend reading anyway.

Good art routines involve activities similar to music:

1. Warm-up sketch
2. Study
3. Current project
4. Decompressing transition

The point of the routine during work time is to ensure your time is used wisely for both growth and progress as well as to avoid losing time in transition.

Macro and Meta Processes

Here is where things begin to get complicated.

The **macro-process** involves managing creative output not at the daily level, but at the level of your projects as well as the cycle of multiple projects. If you have never finished a project before, expect a lot of growing pains in this area, even if you have a daily routine down and working for you.

Going back to the visual arts, creating a painting might involve three phases:

1. Sketch or plan of the work
2. Color study or studies
3. Full painting

Being able to execute this sequence over and over will net a large catalogue of high-quality paintings, even if you are working rather slowly.

Bigger projects like a comic book require more complicated phases:

1. Scriptwriting
2. Storyboarding, sketching, paneling/dialogue plans
3. Pencils
4. Inks
5. Colors
6. Letters
7. Revisions
8. Publication

That last phase, publication, could be a big one, especially if you are independent, involving formatting the comic, transmitting it to the printer, marketing it, and possibly shipping the books to stores or customers (maybe that could be a final phase – fulfillment).

Publishing a book involves four phases:

1. Planning
2. Drafting
3. Revision

4. Publication

Most people think writing is just phase two, the drafting phase, but in reality, writing is all four of these phases. You need to plan your book as well as your process, you need to actually put the words to paper (drafting), then you need to revise and refine your work, and finally, you need to do the complicated publication phase.

Writing a book or putting out a comic is such a huge project, especially for those who have no experience with the macro process, that many people get lost somewhere along the way, abandoning their comic because they didn't realize they needed a script to start, or getting writer's block because they didn't plan out the story for their novel ahead of time.

Skipping steps or not understanding the macro can set you back in terms of both time and money. I've seen artists lose months of productivity in failing to manage their macro process and end up with very upset customers when they mess up the publication process.

Producing an album has a similarly daunting macro structure:

1. Composition
2. Pre-production rehearsal
3. Pre-production recording (demo)
4. Primary production and recording
5. Mixing/editing
6. Mastering
7. Publication/distribution/marketing

Even today, when it is possible to cut several steps (like pre-production rehearsal and recording, artifacts from when you used to have to rent expensive studios by the hour), recording an album is a very big undertaking.

Existing at an even larger level is the management of the entire creative operation, including the cycle of multiple projects and what (if anything) happens between projects. If the project is the macro-process, this is the **meta-process** – the process of processes. For a serious musical act, the end of an album would also be the beginning of a tour cycle in support of that album, which would end and signal the beginning of the album recording cycle yet again. Of course, there are music videos you need to somehow produce within that process.

In the realm of writing, the meta involves planning things like series, where and when you will construct short fiction, how you will market books, how projects will overlap, and how you will interact with your readership.

For someone like me, who does projects across various forms of media, the meta is often in flux. When I come out with a book, I have to both promote the book by producing content across the internet and I have to begin the next book cycle. In fact, I try to put starting my next work as close to finishing the last one as possible, sometimes even beginning my next project before my current one goes live.

The reason? Something that is very disruptive to the meta-process: post-project depression.

Post-project depression

This is a very real phenomenon I have experienced myself and you probably have as well. When you finally complete a long-term goal, whether it is something like a book or something else significant, such as finishing college, it is very common to feel an emotional high that quickly turns around and becomes an emotional low.

I think there are a few reasons for this. First, any emotional high is going to make "returning to normal" feel like a letdown. Second, when all your self is invested in something, completing that thing is the same as losing it. It no longer occupies your mind. It no longer gives you *purpose*, and so a sense of emptiness sets in.

This is why managing your process at the meta-level is critical. Starting your next project right after you finish your previous one will keep that driven part of yourself focused on something important.

This has the added bonus of making you less focused on the reception of your previous project. It may seem odd to want to dull your receptiveness to feedback – after all, you've worked hard, and you want your work to have an impact on others, but such detachment is in practice very beneficial. When you've put your whole self into something, having any response other than glowing praise is going to feel like a spiritual attack. It's only with a little bit of disconnect from that project that you can healthily receive criticism about it or be at peace with some people not liking it.

Something else you can do to avoid depression is to actively engage in the consumption of art, something else that I consider a key to prolific creativity, and I will cover in detail in chapter 8. Giving yourself a "vacation" after finishing a significant work, in which you consume the things you love, will inspire you to get to work on your next project in addition to being an enjoyable activity on its own.

Show your results to the world

The final part of any creative process is publication. I personally do not see any point in working to create a profound work of art without the intention of putting it out into the world to affect and inspire others.

Public display of your work is a very frightening idea if you have never put out your work to strangers, but it is absolutely necessary for both the sense of completion to feel real and for personal growth. Some people undoubtedly will not like what you did, but what is more important is seeing that there are people who enjoyed it and found value. Early on, those who enjoy your work are going to be the ones who point you to what is special about your approach.

In my experience, highly negative reviews say little about the product and are not constructive at all; instead, they are emotive and reactionary, thus they tend to create an emotional reaction for the creator. The most useful critical reviews are those that are mid-line since they will usually include what points of strength your art has. Those are the things you want to focus on cultivating.

The point is, though, that you must go through the risk of showing off what you've accomplished, or else it will be like it never existed at all. Your creations deserve to live!

Alternatives to Routine

For some people, a routine is sub-optimal. For instance, a touring musician may have trouble composing on the road. If you are in the military, deployment will be a major obstacle to any sort of creative productivity. For other people, routine feels too oppressive to feel creative with, though if that is you I urge you to still attempt a routine approach for at least a few weeks or months. What else is there, though?

One option in the face of routine difficulty is the concept of a "sprint" or what I call the "Boot Camp Mindset."

The Boot Camp Mindset

You can tolerate almost anything for a short amount of time. Tolerance of discomfort is largely a function of time, not intensity.

As a creative, you can engage in short-term bouts of extreme work. Michael Moorcock famously could write a book over a weekend; Robert Jordan supposedly could write a book over his spring break.

You can also see this at work when you see an established, experienced band write and record a full album in a matter of weeks. Sammy Haggar recorded the album *I Never Said Goodbye* in 10 days in order to fulfill corporate obligations, freeing him to join Van Halen.

When you engage in a sprint like this, it *must* be for a short amount of time. Generally, I think six weeks is the upper limit for extreme schedules, low sleep, and high work hours with intense focus. I arrived at this window based on the practices of militaries around the world, who almost always limit their highly intensive training programs to six weeks. This is why I call it the boot camp mindset – you are committing to a short-term but intensive program.

I've pushed this six-week limit personally to get projects shipped at a certain time, but that is always followed by a transition to some other focus. Some artists I've talked to run this way all the time. They write for six or eight weeks out of the year, and otherwise are doing other things... or nothing at all.

If you attempt a sprint, and especially if you attempt one when you have a lot of time on your hands, such as during a vacation, be aware that having the focus necessary to be productive is difficult to maintain. Trying to work for eight hours straight is more difficult than trying to work for 2 hours 4 times during the day. Plan to adjust your process during a sprint and pay attention to what things in your temporary routine are working and what things are not.

What is certain though is that during a sprint you have to be working not only consistently, but relentlessly. There is no sprint if you don't show up every day.

Chapter 3: Establish Effective Goals

Earlier, I wrote about establishing goals as part of a work routine. Now it is time to deal with setting goals in general. These can include:

1. Goals for project completion
2. Goals for completion time
3. Career goals
4. Sales goals

Goals are usually what gets people into the game to begin with. Saying to yourself "I want to be an author!" or "I want to be a professional musician!" may speak to your spirit, but I intend to convince you that these are not the right kind of goals for a prolific creator and to show you a few better ways to formulate your goals, both long-term and short term.

You might have heard of SMART goals out in the corporate or education world. As silly as some informational acronyms are, SMART goals make a lot of sense and are a good place to start when it comes to formulating the right kind of goals. Most often SMART stands for:

> **S**pecific
> **M**easurable
> **A**chievable
> **R**elevant
> **T**ime-bound

I've seen other variations (like "results-based" for "R"), but these variations don't detract from the overall purpose of this type of goal-setting. If we look at one of the earlier goals, something like "I want to be a professional musician," we can see it is missing some important information:

1. **What does it mean to be a "professional musician"?**
2. **How will you know when you have achieved the goal?**
3. **Is it even realistic to consider doing music professionally?**
4. **How long should it take to reach the goal?**

Though it is clear there are some problems with this goal, I don't think it is wise to just discard big ideas and grand thoughts. Being a professional is more of a mission, not a goal, and should be there to inspire you to set goals, rather than being something nebulous hanging over your head, reminding you that you can't achieve something. That's one of the big problems with big goals – when we fail to achieve them, we lose heart.

Let's take goals in the creative context a little bit further.

Tasks, Goals, and Missions

First, let's categorize our outcomes:

1. **Tasks** – these are the little things that you set out to do on a daily or weekly basis. Sub-project goals, daily work goals, and social media content fit into this category. Tasks are either completed or abandoned within the short time frame they are necessary. As such, relevance to larger goals is of the most importance.
2. **Projects** – these are your project goals, or the bigger things you will seek to accomplish over a longer period, from a few days to a few months, or perhaps

even longer. A book is a goal, as is a record, a substantive painting, a stage performance of a play or opera, or a film. It's imperative when you set this sort of goal that you attempt to limit the time you will work on it, or else you risk losing your ability to reach completion.

3. **Missions** – these are the really big ideas and career-level goals. If you want to not just write a book, but be a writer who earns his income by his craft, you have a mission. It is imperative goals at this larger level be both achievable and that they have a very clear metric for measurement. After all, at what point is one a "writer"? You should, before you set out, set up some clear criterion for judgment, such as a yearly gross income or a certain number of published works.

Defining Success and Failure

The next step in goal creation is to define how you will know whether you will have met the goal or not, and just as importantly, *when* you should meet it. Time-bounding a goal is very important for defining *failure*. If your goal is to run a mile in under ten minutes, at one point have you failed your goal? A week? A month? Your whole life?

An example of a task-oriented goal would be:

I am going to play through all of my scales today at 140 BPM.

This defines success and, because that definition is time-bound and precise, it also defines failure. If, at the end of the day, you haven't gone through all of your scales, or some of them you are still unable to play at 140 beats-per-minute, you have failed the goal. Anything above 140 BPM counts as success. You can have the same task for the next day, repeat the task or (in the case of failure) attempt the task again.

Let's continue with a project-oriented goal:

I am going to finish the rough draft of this book by February 1st.

This defines success as completion of one of the project steps and is time-bounded. What do you do if you fail this task? In this case, you probably shouldn't just give up, but attempt to finish as quickly as possible.

And let's look at a mission:

I am going to make one thousand dollars per month selling books by 2025.

Again, this is time-bound. However, failure at this stage can mean lots of things. Is this a signal to you that you need to find another career? What are you going to do if you have success (Keep building? Rest?) and what are you going to do about failure? These are questions only you can answer for yourself. This is why long-term mission goals should be approached with a looser touch than those for your day or a project.

Connecting Goals and Methods

Failure should not be viewed as a negative per se. Failure is a chance to evaluate *why* you failed, and to make necessary corrections to your processes that will, in the future, eliminate that failure or get yourself closer to success. Failing at a goal does not make you a failure. Truthfully, failing is one of the very best teachers, as it points directly to those things that you need to improve. If something is working, it probably doesn't need to be fixed, after all.

To this point, consider that goals and processes should always align with one another. The success or failure of the goal is a direct reflection on the process used to attain that goal. That is to say, you should always judge your process by its outcomes, rather than by how you feel about it *while* you are doing it.

After all, it's easier to walk a mile than to run that same mile, but one will get you into better shape than the other.

Consider the above task-oriented goal, "*I am going to play through all of my scales today at 140 BPM.*" If you fail to achieve this task, you can alter something about your process and try the next day. Or, you can consider that the process was fine, but you had set an unrealistic goal. Perhaps you can get through all of your scales at 120 BPM and then increase your goal speed the next week.

If your process is not giving you the improvement you need after several cycles, it is time to change it, especially if you have re-adjusted your goals and looked into other solutions (such as fixing flawed technique in the scale example). We can take the same task and create a goal with a longer term of completion out of it:

I am going to play through all of my scales at 140 BPM at the end of next week.

If you still fail to meet the goal, it is time to adjust your approach. Take a step back and look up some different methods for practicing scales. Maybe you need to try speed bursts or some other method to get you over the hump and to your target speed. Perhaps you need to drop other tasks and spend all your time on scales for a few days. When you have this kind of feedback, it is good to take a step back and evaluate your routine.

When it comes to project goals, the same basic principles apply. If you wanted to finish a book by a certain date, why did you fail? Is it because you didn't spend enough hours working? Is it because you didn't set a realistic goal? Does your routine need to be updated to improve transitions? Or, is your process fine, but you realized half-way through the draft one of your ideas didn't work and you needed to start over?

Very long-term goals, especially those related to careers, can benefit from ongoing evaluations of the processes *before* you reach the time boundary. If you aim to make one thousand dollars per month by a certain date, and it is apparent you are very far from your goal before you reach the date, you should be evaluating what you are doing to reach that goal.

If you aren't making enough money selling books, why are you failing? Is there something you should be doing, but aren't? Do you need to learn more about advertising? Are you writing books that are proven to sell, or writing books without concern for the market while *hoping* you make money? Have you written enough to justify making one thousand dollars per month? How many books do authors making that much money have for sale?

I like the money-making example because many new authors have very unrealistic expectations about how much money they will make in this business, as well as just how much work it takes to make money. They think that their book will magically take off and be a best-seller, without realizing that there is no market for the amphibian romance novel they worked so hard to publish. Authors are often unwilling to look at what others have done to make money and try that method for themselves, or they refuse to use such methods because they consider them unsavory in some way (authors tend to hate being marketers. It makes them – or us, I should say – feel dirty).

Being able to recognize a failure in such a goal, and just as importantly, identify why you failed, will save a lot of heartache and will also allow for tremendous growth over time. Each time you fail, you are honing your process, making it better and more effective, as well as adjusting your mindset so you can be happier and more successful.

Wording Your Goals for Success

The best way to format a goal is to put all of the above together:

> *I am going to do X by Y time. I am going to do Z to achieve it.*

Now everything is there and easy to evaluate as well as visualize clearly. We can even at this point connect everything from the mission all the way down to the individual tasks in one big, well-defined, process-oriented goal.

> *I am going to make one thousand dollars per month selling books by 2025. I am going to write three books per year to do it. I will write one thousand words per day to write three books per year.*

Mission goal supported by project goals supported by task goals.

I like the above goal because it hammers home the importance of the process, and why I put processes before goals. If you write one thousand words per day, every day, you can finish three books per year. If you write three books per year over five years, you have fifteen books to sell. If you sell one copy of each book per day at an average of $2.99 you will be making over 1,300 dollars in sales per month – close to one thousand dollars in net royalties if you publish independently.

Of course, there is more to publishing books than finishing the drafting process, but if you keep your drafting process humming along, suddenly you can, in a few years, do what most people can't even imagine – write not just one book, but *fifteen* books, and can even make some good passive income doing it. 1,000 dollars isn't enough to live on (for most people), but it *is* realistic and achievable if you stick to the process.

One thousand words per day isn't even very much. As you skill up, you'll soon move past that task goal and be able to be even more productive. The same consistency at 2,000 words per day could potentially double your output, and significantly increase your income as part of your mission.

You can apply this same goal-setting to any career, really, as long as you can break down the steps for the mission into projects and finally the regular tasks that will be your daily focus.

Don't Lose Sight of the Big Picture

Even though you have better goals now, don't forget about why you got into your field. Don't give up on your dreams – your mission.

Keeping that mission fixed in your mind is excellent inspiration and will make any daily grind more tolerable. Whenever you have a hard time working, just think of the mission, and how your work is tangibly moving you closer to that ultimate goal.

Then it's not really like work, because you are achieving your mission. The small-scale work *is* making your dream a reality.

Chapter 4 – The Growth Mindset

Failure, as I mentioned, is an opportunity for growth. It is the most important opportunity for growth, but it is certainly not the only opportunity, nor should you wait for a failure to instigate growth. Growth is a necessary part of creation and becomes increasingly important the longer you persist in any medium.

Classical Guitar – a short anecdote

A few years ago, I put out a reflection video talking about why I abandoned the classical guitar. I didn't stop playing the instrument completely, but I stopped being a "classical guitarist" and doing all the things that classical guitarists usually do, like practicing the standard repertoire and performing it.

There were lots of responses to that video – far more than I anticipated – but the most common reaction was one of hostility or bewilderment. There were people who couldn't seem to understand why I would just drop something that had been so central to my life and something through which I had earned a living for a decade. Some thought it had to be because I was bad (I was in fact very good, hence I could make money playing), others thought it was because I lacked some sort of artistic purity that is endemic to classical guitar.

The latter was probably closest to the truth. There were lots of reasons, including my deteriorating hearing, but the main reason I abandoned "classical guitar" was because of malaise born of out overwhelming boredom.

Originally, I enjoyed the technical challenge of playing the repertoire. It spurred huge musical growth and helped me to grow as an artist. Then, I enjoyed taking my guitar out and making money with it. I enjoyed teaching guitar at the college level and to individual students.

After a while, though, it became an empty experience. I cared nothing for the music I played because I had not completely created it myself. I felt no special purpose. Did the world *really* need me to record and perform the same guitar pieces every other academic player has learned over the last thirty years? Was there really anywhere else to go in this field?

Practicing became a burden simply because it pointed to nothing for me.

I had stagnated, and I longed for growth. I tried a lot of other things, but I struggled to work outside the classical area. It's very hard to form a decent band, and as a classical guitarist, I could always make money by myself. It was all under my control, and it was hard to abandon something that had both once given me purpose and continued to give me money.

So it was that when I turned 29, I decided to abandon music and become a writer. I threw my whole self into the endeavor, playing guitar only occasionally to upload videos to YouTube, where I wanted people with modest means to be able to learn music for free – the original motivation for the creation of my YouTube channel.

It was one of the best decisions I ever made, but the transition was very painful. I had a lot of self-identity still tied to music, and I ended up still working in music as a public-school teacher after that, which was like a reminder that I couldn't ever fully escape my prison.

Eventually, I did return to music and recorded an ambient rock album called *Memories Adrift* mostly by myself. I really would not have been able to do it had I not had the very painful transition away from classical music. I had to grow a lot to be able to just go back and do simple compositions again. It was my mindset that needed adjusting, not my technique.

Growth is usually painful

Growing hurts.

I remember as a child complaining to my father that my shins hurt. He said it was growing pain, and that it meant I was getting bigger. This was years before I learned about the pain of bodybuilding.

It hurts to grow physically.

It also hurts to grow intellectually and spiritually.

You should have a mindset that not only accepts this pain as proper and expected, but actively seeks it out.

Bodybuilding – an anecdote

When I was 27 I moved to Las Vegas. My father had been killed the previous year in a workplace incident, and the trauma of that loss had hit my family hard.

I was still teaching. I was still playing guitar. I knew I needed a big change. I got a phone call asking if I could take a position in Las Vegas in ten days. I agreed.

When I got to Sin City I weighed close to 300 pounds. Years of negligence and outright abuse had taken their toll on my body. There was a gym in my apartment complex, and somehow, I got the itch to turn my body around. I think the inception was a video on YouTube from Scooby – an infamous fitness personality that is known for being hyper-honest about everything. He said it would take about five years of work to build thirty or forty pounds of muscle, and that food shouldn't need to taste good, and while that would turn off most people, it inspired me.

That was a challenge, and one that I needed to take.

The job I had when I got to Vegas was not what I was promised. I had about half the work I was supposed to have, and that meant I had to live my life very lean financially. I had no money for a social life. However, since there was little work in the way of hours, I also had a lot of free time on my hands.

It was a perfect environment for incredible growth.

Oddly, I didn't grow much as a musician, despite my best efforts. I did grow in terms of my body. I grew as a writer, too, but that's not where I spent most of my focus and effort.

I went to the gym every day, sometimes twice, for hours at a time. I honed my diet through countless iterations. I was sore and hungry every day for months on end.

Within two years I had transformed my body into something much closer to the ideal.

I learned three important lessons from the entire effort:

1. You *are* what you *do* repeatedly.
2. Everything is completed one step at a time.
3. Discomfort is not something to avoid.

My current creative process was definitely influenced by my fitness routine. Crafting an attractive body was the result of steps; I knew completing other large projects, like books, would happen the same way. I was able to, with my room-mate, also complete several screenplays by the time I left, and many of those days working on those projects were painful but necessary.

Growth or Decay – there is no standing still

This is another harsh reality of both biology and spirit: **if you are not growing, you are decaying**.

Life grows, it reaches its zenith, then it begins to age – to decay. This is a natural process that our culture is very concerned with halting, but one of the things I learned from my intense focus on the physical is that it is true on smaller time scales as well.

If you are hitting the gym hard you will grow. You will get stronger. Your muscles will get physically larger and more robust. When you stop stressing your body in this way, you don't stand still. You begin to shrink and get weaker.

When things come to a halt, they don't stay frozen. They go backward.

Plantar Fasciitis – an anecdote

Toward the end of my time in Las Vegas, I had learned a great deal about my body – enough to know that taking bodybuilding further than I had would either yield very little results for the increased effort as I approached my natural peak, or I would need to start taking steroids. The reality was that most of the fitness models that are used to sell gym memberships and supplements are "enhanced" athletes.

I decided to re-align my goals toward general fitness and changed my focus toward more cardiovascular intensive exercise routines. Again, I saw lots of growth, and got even more fit and lean than I had been prior. This wasn't going to last, though.

When my wife went into labor with our first child, I made a stupid decision and, instead of putting on my work boots to take her to the hospital, I put on an older pair of running shoes that I thought would be comfortable.

My wife was in labor for twenty-four hours (without drugs, by the way) and there was nowhere in the delivery room for me to sit. I stood for twenty-four hours straight in worn-out shoes. I didn't feel the repercussions of this immediately, but (not to take anything away from my wife, who certainly suffered more than I did) within a few days I would find it almost impossible to walk or even stand.

I developed plantar fasciitis in both of my feet. Not only that, but I had to start a new job when my son was just five days old. It was also a teaching job, requiring me to be on my feet for a minimum of six hours per day, and included me walking across a very large campus twice.

I did everything I could to try to make it through those early days – I put special insoles into my dress shoes, I sat down as much as I could, and I iced and heated the arches of my feet whenever possible during the day.

It forced me to rethink everything. I couldn't exercise – or at least, I couldn't do the exercise I been doing for two years. I couldn't even walk without experiencing intense pain, and I couldn't take any time off. I ended up gaining almost thirty pounds in the six months after my son was born, erasing years' worth of work on my body, which I thought was important.

I decayed.

When I was finally able to get back into the gym, I had trouble doing a single pull-up.

Change Something Once a Year

When I was forced to rethink my body, I also rethought the other things in my life.

I rethought my YouTube channel and turned it into an analysis and commentary channel, rather than focusing on guitar instruction (guitar stuff wasn't popular).

I rethought my approach to writing and publishing, and eventually self-published my first book (a samurai tale called *Muramasa: Blood Drinker*) in 2016.

I rethought the purpose of exercise in my life. 2015-2016 was some of the biggest growth I had ever had in my life. I reflected and realized that each year prior to that had been equally huge in terms of growth. That is also when I noticed that every single year of my life had held within it some gigantic change.

Growth in every area of my life was spurred on by huge stresses, big changes, and those changes forced the severing of ingrained habits.

This became a bit of a personal philosophy for me – change something big about your life every year.

It has to be something big. We're not talking about switching from wheat bread to rye here, we're talking about something that makes you totally re-organize your static routines, your mindset, and your understanding of your goals. What I mean is things like changing your job, where you live, who you work for, what genre you write in, your entire wardrobe, etc. You could also get married or have a child.

Even something like switching up your workout routine or getting a dog can spur growth.

Here are some big changes that happened to me (in order):

Switched my musical focus to classical guitar performance

Left academia

Moved cities

My father was killed

Moved cities again – this time to Las Vegas

Changed my body

Moved again within Las Vegas

Switched creative careers to writing

Moved again to Los Angeles

Switched my day job to public school teaching

Within one month: Bought a house, got married, moved cities again

Had a child

Changed the focus of my writing career

Quit my day job

Moved again

Had a second child

Started writing nonfiction!

The only place where I really stagnated (or moved backward) was in 2018 before my wife and I decided to buy a different house. It had been more than a year without a big change – I had quit my day job a year prior and was spinning my wheels in multiple places after a huge beginning to the year. The move was probably the most stressful move I ever did – partially because I had accrued more stuff, partially because I had a child and a pregnant wife to worry about while we sold one house and bought another.

The shock was what I needed, though, and it made me realign things. I was able to quickly write and publish an experimental type of book, something I would repeat after the birth of my daughter to some unexpected success. The wheels were turning again. I was able to quickly cut some weight that had been sticking around for more than a year.

Then my daughter was born.

Final Fantasy with Aurelia – an anecdote

The birth of my daughter was another huge blessing – and a huge stressor. My wife had suffered a difficult pregnancy but an easy birth (as far as such things go). Aurelia, as we named her, had her own stresses.

She suffered from infant reflux due to a mechanically weak esophageal sphincter. This is something she grew out of, but for the weeks following her birth, she couldn't sleep unless she was being held upright. That meant my wife and I had to sleep in shifts and sit in an easy chair holding the baby so she could rest. Because of the mechanics of holding a tiny human, I couldn't do much besides hold her. The only things I could reasonably do were read on a phone or kindle, or, as I discovered, play on the Nintendo Switch.

This was due to Nintendo's odd design choice when it came to their controllers. The joy-cons that come with the system can be held one in each hand and used as a single typical controller. I hadn't realized until those days that such a choice could be a blessing for people who suffer from physical disabilities that make holding a traditional controller uncomfortable or impossible.

During this time my work also came to a halt, somewhat expectedly. I had anticipated the difficulty of dealing with a young baby and recovering mother and thus appropriately set up my latest book release and my social media schedule to compensate. I hadn't anticipated that I would get no work done at all, but that it is what happened.

This turned out to be a kind of blessing because it forced me to grow yet again. I had been working relentlessly for years at this point, going so far as to take a laptop or guitar with me on every vacation I ever took so I could work on the road. Now, I simply couldn't work.

I could read and play games, though.

After talking to a friend about it, I decided to buy the Final Fantasy VII port for the Switch, considering I hadn't really touched it since the 90s. It's a game lots of people have a great deal of affection for, but I had never latched onto in the same way (I'm a big JRPG fan, but I liked other games in the series much more). I had learned a lot about analysis between my teen years and my thirties, so it was actually a very enjoyable experience – approaching the game from the perspective of "How does this game work? Why do so many people love it?"

Those little controllers were also a blessing for my wife, because she did some of the same things with some other games.

It is rare that I purposefully set aside large portions of time to consume media that I enjoy, whether it is movies, games, or books, and my daughter's inability to sleep had forced me to do just that. It was an exhausting experience in many ways, but it was also the first vacation I had taken in a very long time – a vacation where I truly let go of my impulse to work and just recharged my mind and spirit.

There are definitely worse things than holding babies.

I also decided to take the same analytical approach I took to Final Fantasy to some other things and read some books far outside of my normal genres (specifically *Twilight,* much to the chagrin of my YouTube subscribers). That experience made me grow, too.

Sometimes growth happens against your will (perhaps it mostly happens against your will, but that is another discussion). Sometimes you grow in ways you don't expect.

Always Be Growing

So here's everything I have to say about growth put simply:

1. Growth happens through stress.
2. If you aren't growing, you are decaying
3. Seek out growth when necessary, embrace big changes when they are forced on you.
4. Failure is an opportunity for growth.

So:

Don't avoid failure. Don't avoid stress. Don't be afraid to take some risks.

Chapter 5 – The Professional Mindset

I questioned earlier what it means to be a professional, but even if being a professional isn't an explicit goal of yours, you should *act* as a professional. In fact, you should as quickly as possible jettison all feelings of being an "amateur" from your language and your very mind no matter where you are on your creative journey.

Be a professional.

This means much more than "making money," or similar materialistic outcomes. This means treating yourself is if you are good enough to do the job you set out to do and you are good enough to get paid to do it. It also means you respect those who are employing you enough to do the best job you can do with your resources and treat other professionals with the same due respect.

From that position, it is very easy to determine what constitutes "amateur" behavior and avoid it. To go one step further, you should probably also avoid amateurs in general.

Let's dig a bit deeper.

Two Mindsets

I like to contrast what I consider the *Professional Mindset* with what I call the *Amateur Mindset*.

An amateur has a set of self-actualizing views about himself. Here are a few examples:

1. I'm not good enough to earn money

2. I'd like to be good one day
3. I'm an aspiring writer
4. I'd feel embarrassed to show this to people
5. This guy is my idol!
6. I wish I could play like he does!
7. I'm not sure what I'm best at.

A professional has what amounts to the opposite view of themselves. Here are some examples:

1. I deserve to get paid for my work
2. I'm good at what I do
3. I'm a writer.
4. It's hard limiting my portfolio to just a few good pieces
5. I appreciate his art. I even learned a few things by analyzing it.
6. What a great piece! I think I'll learn it.
7. I'm very good at these things… perhaps I could be great at more things…

Yes, professionals are always growing. It's not an arrival point, but a mindset, or a way of doing things.

Let's Jam – the Amateur Mindset

One of the first things I learned in the world of music is that amateurs and professionals have vastly different approaches to interacting with other musicians.

This is all too common an experience:

You run into some cool folks at a party or a show, and you get invited to come over and "jam." A few days later, you pack your gear into your car, unload it at the new friend's house, and start warming up.

You ask what everyone wants to play.

Nobody knows. Everyone knows a few songs, but no two people know the same song.

You start goofing off and talking about what kind of music everyone likes. The drummer likes Kiss. You like Sabbath. Not too far off. The bass player likes Korn. You cringe inwardly, but decide to teach everyone "Paranoid" while you all have some beers.

That gets boring, so you play a riff you came up with and the drummer plays along to it for a while. The other guitarist is lost on the chords, so he tries to solo on top of it using an E minor pentatonic scale – the only one he learned from *Guitar Player* magazine.

You decide it was a good time. Maybe you guys should be a band.

You call everyone the next week. Some people are busy, so you wait another week and meet up on a Saturday two weeks later to jam some more.

The bassist mentions his girlfriend is a good singer.

Next time, she shows up. She doesn't know what to sing over your riff. You come up with some words that she doesn't like.

You drink some more. That helps.

The bassist comes up with another riff. It sounds like Korn.

After getting drunker, things start to sound okay.

You spend the next week trying to herd the group together. The drummer is just not available. The other guitarist suggests a friend of his, but you all met at the first drummer's house, so maybe it's really his band. Worse, you left your amp over there...

Amateurs jam. Professionals rehearse.

In the music space, this says it all. When you first start out as a musician, especially in the rock genres, you will encounter lots of other musicians that are interested in "jamming." This usually involves getting together and attempting to get music to emerge from an amorphous, unstructured interaction.

In other words, it's unproductive.

Let's be clear, though – improvisation and "conversational playing" have an important place in the genres of jazz and blues, however, amateur musicians imagining starting up a rock or pop project seldom have a jazz background. In truth, jazz is highly structured. There is lots of improvisation, but usually over a standard set of chords and a melody that is decided upon by the group. Only the most extreme forms of jazz, such as free jazz, eschew this fundamental grounding to give way to the improvisational work.

Jamming doesn't make you a free jazz player.

Free Jazz artists are generally well versed in the more standard practice, which gives a huge language set for the interaction of the artists. I say this as a musician with huge amounts of improvisational experience, including free jazz performance. I should also note that free jazz is usually not very popular.

What does this all mean? You'll find out through experience if you are a musician, but most amateurs don't have enough of an idea of what they are doing to jump into an improvisational setting and produce something worthwhile.

When jazz musicians intend to record or perform, they *rehearse.* They get together, decide on what they are going to perform (often decided by a bandleader), practice it together, and then get on with the recording or performance.

This is the same for musicians in less improvisational genres as well.

Amateurs invite their friends into the garage and hope they will become the next Beatles.

Professionals assemble a band of like-minded artists to compose and perform music with specific goals and a musical direction in mind. More than that, they've probably composed their own music or decided on their repertoire before they ever start inviting others to fill out their group.

So, what should you do if you want to operate as a professional?

You have to learn to say "No" a lot. If there is no goal, you should pass on jamming. If the goal is different from your own artistic goals, you should probably pass, but you may want to participate for career reasons; you'll have to be the judge.

Approaching things as an amateur will usually cause you to waste your time. Acquiescing to amateurs will also suck your time away, so be a professional and work only with other professionals if you value your time and want to create artistic outputs with any sort of reasonable time investment.

Working With Others

The above lesson can be transcribed to a variety of other media. Are you a comic artist? Work with a professional writer, not an "aspiring" writer. The inverse is true for writers

– work with competent, professional artists, not wannabes. Are you a filmmaker? Work with legitimate cinematographers, actors, and production staff. Don't hire wannabes.

Are you a wannabe? Stop it.

When it comes to working with others, you should always have the end goals agreed upon by both of you. What is this project? Where is it heading? How do we know we have completed it? How long until we complete this project? What does the workflow for each of us look like?

You should also be upfront about money. Is one person bearing the financial responsibility and hiring all others? This is common in the comics industry, where one person on the project, such as the writer, will act as the publisher and hire artists, colorists, letterers, editors, and anyone else either for a set fee or else negotiate royalties with each of them separately. With music – how are royalties going to be handled? Who is managing the band, if anyone? How much are you going to charge for each performance and what is the split?

You will save yourself lots of drama by having all financial aspects out in the open *before* you begin committing to any collaborations. This doesn't mean you have to have every detail in some legalistic contract, but everyone should at least be on the same page as far as financial goals go.

The less drama you have – or really, the more you avoid dramatic collaborations – the more you will spend your time on projects that will reach fruition rather than wither on the vine. You will be much more prolific approaching all partnerships like a professional.

The Problem with Writing Groups

Participation in "writing groups" is something a great many writers, myself included, will experience or have experienced in the past. These are either formal or informal gatherings of writers with the purpose of reading and giving feedback to the group members on their writing.

This has the possibility of offering a cheap way to improve your writing, especially early on: you get feedback from several other people, and you also have deadlines to push you toward goal completion (and deadlines can be very helpful, as I will detail later). However, these sorts of pursuits are often counter-productive when you consider the alternatives.

First, in a writing group, you are treating yourself as an amateur who is blind to his skill without external feedback and whose time is worthless. Second, you are dealing with a group of people who are likewise in the amateur mindset. It's the blind leading the blind, and very often each person is trying to blindly walk in a different direction, since it is rare to have a group of writers who all want to write in the same genre.

When you think of spending your time in a writing group, consider alternatives:

1. Rather than spending time reading the work of amateurs, you should be reading the work of professionals to learn their effective techniques.

2. Rather than getting feedback from readers who aren't knowledgeable of your genre and who aren't experts in the craft, you could get feedback from an expert in both your genre and your craft: an established editor.

3. Rather than spending your time meeting with other people who have different publication goals than you, you could be writing.

Yes, it costs money to hire an editor, but if your time is valuable (and it is), that should be an acceptable trade-off if you feel you need that guidance and feedback to improve your manuscript. Remember, a professional values his or her time, since time is money. Likewise, he will consider the time of other professionals to be of value as well.

Like many things, there is an absolute value to being part of a critique group, but what is more important is the comparative value. Compared to doing something else (like I suggest), is it a benefit, or a loss? Is the group of a high enough quality that you, along with all the others, are getting a solid benefit from participation?

How to be Professional

Nobody is perfect and sometimes life gets in the way of productivity, but you should endeavor to meet all of these maxims:

1) **Work for payment.** That means no "free" work unless that free work is explicitly tied to something else that is providing value for you. A free book on Amazon should be building your email list, generating reviews for future monetization, or selling a future book in the series. If you are a musician, you should get paid for sitting in with a band. If you go to an open mic night it should be to sell tickets to a concert, or some other monetization. Free art distributed online should be building your commission business. One of your

end goals should be earning a return on your time investment.

2) **Deliver on time.** If you have a time-bounded task or deadline, you should be meeting that deadline every single time that you aren't impaired by something truly significant – don't miss deadlines because you have a cold. If you miss a deadline, it should be near miss. There should *never* be a case where you can't deliver the product at all (just a tip – if you *can* set a deadline, set it at least a week or two *after* you think you'll be done, just in case you get the flu). If you crowdfund your project, you have customers that deserve their item when you agreed to give it to them – don't make them regret supporting you!

3) **Treat others like they are professionals and expect others to act professionally toward you**. Save the drama for your mama. Pay your collaborators on time and in full. Don't work with amateurs who suck up your time. Don't tolerate flakes. Don't work with people who miss deadlines and make you look bad by association. Do not tolerate parties who are inconsistent with payment.

4) **Present yourself as a professional to the customers and audience.** Look the part. Talk the part. Don't show up drunk or high to gigs. Don't act like an amateur who doesn't value the time of others. Have confidence in the tasks you know you can do and be upfront with your skills when

collaborating with others. Avoid dramatic entanglements.

5) **Use the appropriate tools.** Invest in high-grade gear that can get the job done – this includes software. Don't use the free alternative just because it is free. If photoshop is the industry standard, use it. Artists shouldn't be inking with Bic pens, but with quality india ink and good brushes. Musicians shouldn't be showing up with the amp that came with their first guitar. In fact, all guitarists reading this have my official permission to buy a high-quality tube amplifier!

6) **Produce a great product.** This is the most important thing of all. You should give every project your full confidence and effort, with the intention of making the best it possibly can be. It should stand side-by-side with the work of other professionals and have full value. If it doesn't stand up, then work hard to improve and get as close as you can to your ideal standard with each attempt.

Why You Should Be a Professional

Not *act* like a professional; *be* a professional.

You should adopt this mindset because it will enhance what you are doing. Others will perceive you differently. You will perceive *yourself* differently. Adopting this attitude will be a constant reminder to yourself that you are very serious about what you are doing, that you are endeavoring to succeed, and that you are worthy of success.

You are what you repeatedly do, so being professional will turn you into a professional.

You can try the following experiment if you doubt me:

Put on a suit (or professional dress) every time you intend to work, whether it is going to a practice room, sitting down to draw or paint, sitting down to write, etc. Do it consistently for at least a week.

I've done this in several environments, and it works. First, when you go into a practice room (or wherever), you are wearing a reminder that you are there to work, not goof off. Looking at your hands and seeing cuffs there will make it crystal clear what you should be doing if your focus begins to wane.

Second, other people will magically treat you better. They will treat you like a professional because you look like a professional. That, in turn, will feedback into your self-image and make you live up to those people's perceptions of you.

If you look out of place, don't let it bother you. You're just trying this for a week, after all, and if it doesn't work, dressing well won't do you any career harms. Moreover, I discovered that, at least as a man, it's very difficult to be overdressed. When you dress well and everyone else doesn't, you merely make everyone else look like slobs.

I did this at a few different jobs I had teaching guitar lessons at music stores. People who didn't know me assumed that I was the manager or owner. When people came in seeking lessons, they assumed I was the best teacher there because I looked like the best one there. That drove up my business, which gave me more experience in a shorter amount of time, thus making me the best teacher there as a sort of self-fulfilling prophecy.

There is, of course, more to success and professional atti-tude than smart dress (like always showing up on time), but I know my wardrobe had an impact.

The best part?

I got all my first suits for less than 100 dollars total at thrift stores. Men usually get rid of clothes not because they have gone out of style, but because they have grown (sideways) out of them, which means it's easy to get good suits (often worn very little) for a cheap price.

This is not something I do now, but it was a great thing to do at the time. If you feel your wardrobe is light on the pro-fessional attire (and you are a man – it's harder for women), head over to the Goodwill on the nice side of town and see what's there for you.

The Social Media Professional

As an artist in the 21st century, you cannot ignore social media. It is where your audience is. Gone are the days when audience interaction meant walking on stage or showing up to a convention to shake hands and sell books. Now, it is all about the two-way information flow. Just like managing your time on social media, managing the way you act on social me-dia is a balancing act.

Before I go further, let me say that the "wisdom" that you have heard regarding how a professional ought to act on so-cial media is likely the inverse of reality. If you think a profes-sional ought to be polite and neutral, not negative and cer-tainly never crass or insulting on social media, you are dead wrong. Let me explain.

When you are trying to build an audience, and most im-portantly sell a product, you have to gain the attention of people. There are a few ways to do this, but they ultimately boil down to two paths:

1. You create interesting content that people pay attention to.
2. You rent the audience from other people who make interesting content that people pay attention to.

The first path is the more difficult of the two, but it is ultimately the most effective over the long-term, because it not only builds the audience, it creates a means by which you continue to hold their attention.

The second path is advertising. It is expensive and temporary, lasting only as long as you are willing to continue paying for it.

If you want to be polite, neutral, and generally likable, you are going to have to go the second route, because you will be too boring for anyone to care about.

Don't believe me?

Pay attention to headlines. What does every news organization do in their headlines? They sell controversy. They appeal to prejudice. They appeal to anger, outrage, cynicism, and identity.

This is how they gain attention. It is very difficult to gain attention by being positive or wholesome. This is the reality of human nature – we respond to negative emotions with more vigor than positive ones.

This means that the content you produce, especially if it is the realm of ideas such as blog posts or discussion videos, will have a much better chance of grabbing attention if it is "negative" in some way. The popular channels that you end up having to rent are run by the people who understand this.

If I do a negative movie review, it will get 3-5 times the views on average of a positive one, particularly if the video title points to the opinion (like when I say in a title that a movie sucks). It's so lopsided that some viewers complain that I just hate everything, when in fact most of my reviews are positive. They just aren't watching (or aren't being shown by YouTube) any of the positive ones.

However, doing nothing but negative, controversial content will not maintain an audience for an artist. For that, you need content that makes your audience feel good and makes them like you. Also in my experience, people you attract via negativity are in a negative place generally or else will feel negative emotions associated with you, even if they agree with you. They aren't likely to be the positive fans that will approach your art with an expectation that they will like it.

I have followed a strategy that mixes the potent negative content and the less potent positive content for quite a while. The growth is slower, but the audience that sticks around is generally more interested in you than people you pick up purely through negative content.

I put out a few controversial videos per week, talking about things like bad modern movies, politics, problems in the publishing world, social justice, and the actions of big corporations like Disney.

The rest of the week I spend doing things like putting out audiobook chapters or short readings, analyzing pulp fiction, talking logic, talking about heavy metal, and giving writing lectures.

As a concrete example, here are the videos I put out January 19th-25th, 2020:

Sunday: Trans Scifi author CANCELLED by trans mob over pro-trans story?

Monday: All it takes is one complaint to lose your email database

Tuesday: Review – An Encyclopedia of Tolkien by David Day

Wednesday: Livestream (NewPub talk: Conan vs. Elric with Jesse White)

Thursday: MTG Review – Magic Game Night box set

Friday: Storycraft: 10 Ways to Make a Character Likable

Saturday: "Hot" "Girls" for Bernie – Postmodern Beauty in Politics

It was a bit of a wild week, so I did three controversial videos. The rest were positive videos that were also highly targeted toward fantasy fans – people like me and people who are likely to enjoy my fantasy books.

These videos aren't just a way to market, they are a way to develop relationships with viewers, to have the discussions I enjoy having on the internet with people who like similar things to me. Information flows two ways; it's very different from an ad.

The Unkind Internet

There is a downside to putting out controversial content, and it is the fact that you will attract people who hate you as much as you attract people who think the way you do. Just to clarify, "controversial" is context specific. Putting out a video about how much a Star Wars movie sucks is very controversial to one demographic, but is irrelevant to others. Controversial *can* mean political, but not necessarily.

How you deal with haters, trolls, and malcontents is up to you. You can try to convince them (virtually never works), you can engage them in hopes of convincing bystanders (sometimes works), or you can block (always works).

I have different strategies depending on the platform.

A good strategy for twitter (or similar) is to block any random haters (or idiots) that have a small follower count. It's a waste of your time to engage anonymous trolls and sock puppets. If the account has a large following, consider if engaging them will attract their audience. If not, again, you should block them.

Don't ignore; *block or ban.*

It took me far too long to learn this, and there are hours, perhaps *days*, I will never get back because I didn't realize it was pointless to talk to morons and people who wish I was dead.

I take an approach to YouTube that is similar to Twitter, but I tend to ignore a lot more of the noise and let people go at it in the comments section, mostly because there is more to deal with than on other platforms, but I won't hesitate to ban if somebody is being dishonest or annoying to everyone else. If somebody is drifting by your videos to hurl insults at you and everyone else, there is really no downside to banning them; they don't improve your SEO (Search Engine Optimization) with insults and they aren't going to buy anything from you. This approach has significantly improved my experience and made my comment section much more fun to participate in.

If you are a person who loves conflict, feel free to ignore my advice but, as a person who generally is tolerant of conflict, I tend to avoid most of it because it is simply a waste of my time. Some followers are attracted to people who like to dish it out, though, so know thyself and use your best judgment.

I don't believe in being "apolitical" because nobody is actually apolitical, and I don't believe that being "professional" on social media involves shutting up and letting hundreds of people dog pile you.

What you should reject is the notion that blocking someone is *bad*. People who complain about being blocked by people they dislike are complaining about a core feature of the platform. It's there to filter out the noise from the interactions which really matter to the users, and you should use it as a creator. Likewise, trolls will disrupt conversations that you want to have with others (what I call "bell ringing"), so blocking is always better than muting or trying to just ignore the person.

Being professional on social media does not necessarily mean being polite. It *does* mean managing your profiles with your business in mind. That means focusing on your audience, not on trolls; it does *not* mean you have to grin through harassment and abuse.

Chapter 6 – The Farmer Mindset

Also known as "the cows don't care that you're sick."

I realize that for people who didn't grow up in the agriculture industry (as I did), the idea of not taking sick days is a strange concept, but it is a harsh reality in the creative industries. You cannot let minor inconveniences get in the way of delivering your projects on time and under budget.

This doesn't mean *no sick days ever*, but it does mean that your excuses are irrelevant when it comes to hard deadlines. When farming, certain things simply must be done at a certain time or you risk losing lots of money.

You have to prune trees and vines at very particular times. Failure to do so within the right time frame will negatively affect yield. As I write this, it is time to prune the peaches. I must prune my peach tree in the next few days or I risk having a small crop or even having branches break. Things are very busy, but I have to get it done!

If you have a horse that is in labor and you don't attend to it, you could end up with two dead horses.

If you don't harvest your grapes on time, they will wither on the vine in the California heat.

Farming is like that. There are lots of days where there is little to do. Once the crops are going, it's just simple maintenance until harvest time. However, when it's time to work, you *must* work.

Deadlines Matter

You should look at all the deadlines you set for yourself or have imposed upon you has *hard* deadlines. In other words, failing to meet the deadline essentially invalidates the work. The benefit of this approach is that it ensures that you finish your projects and they don't end up in limbo or "development hell." It therefore also forces you to avoid perfectionism (more on that later).

In the publishing world, missing deadlines is a serious setback. It happens, sometimes, for reasons nobody can control, but most things you *can* control. You shouldn't feel bad that you missed a deadline because of a traumatic event; you *should* feel bad if you missed it because you were out partying.

If you miss your pre-order date on Amazon, you will lose your ability to set-up pre-orders for an entire year. For publishing companies and prolific authors, this is a huge deal. Likewise shipping a product that isn't ready will be a big deal. You have to deliver on time and also deliver the product at a high enough quality for it to be successful. Consider how much is at stake for a periodical like a comic book. Failing to finish the art means you miss the ship date for that month, which means the local comic shop is going to have people coming in looking for a book that doesn't exist yet.

I mentioned setting deadlines for yourself. This may seem like odd behavior for an artist like myself, who works completely independently and is beholden to nobody, but I do try to set deadlines for myself regularly.

A deadline hones your focus. It also forces you to think in limited terms and be realistic about your own capabilities. I prefer to adjust my expectations to reality, not try to force reality to conform to my expectations, and deadlines help me stay grounded in this way. If you have a limited time to complete an assignment, you must engage in triage, either at the outset or as you go along, of the various things you want to include in your project.

If you were to put this in software design terms, you would not include features that you couldn't fully implement in the development window.

Software development, or even better game development, is an excellent example of the importance of deadlines and is relevant to this text because it *is* a creative endeavor. As a deadline for a software project looms, the development team has to make decisions about what they can reasonably accomplish before the ship date.

Is there a feature that still doesn't work as intended? Cut it. Is the interface ugly and hard to use? Shift resources to get it fixed. Are the art assets less-than-stellar? Fix only the most visible ones.

Some games are infamous for being stuck in "development hell" due to an inability to set deadlines and focus on core features. *Duke Nukem Forever* was in development for more than ten years and was only released after 3D Realms, the studio developing the game, shut down. Star Citizen has been in development for more than eight years, and there is no release date in sight as of this writing – and yet the feature set seems only to grow.

Strict deadlines help to avoid problems like "feature creep," where you keep adding in features to a piece of software to the point where the core purpose has been either lost or hindered. If you have to ship on a certain date, you're probably going to drop those buggy multiplayer maps and just focus on your campaign (or, since it's 2020, probably the other way around).

Development hell is not unique to software, either. There are notorious books and albums that have been years in the making only to either be abandoned or fail to live up to the effort involved. *Chinese Democracy* by Guns 'n Roses is an excellent example, but far from the only one. As of the writing of this book, fans of *A Song of Ice and Fire* are still patiently waiting for the series conclusion to be released by George R.R. Martin while the TV series based on the unreleased book has already concluded to much backlash.

Just as an aside, this doesn't mean extremely *tight* deadlines are good. If you don't give yourself enough time to reasonably complete a project the way you envision it, then that will cause you more stress than you need and also force you to release an inadequate product. Deadlines should be strict, but appropriate. You'll get better ideas about how to set them as you complete more projects.

What I do usually is to set up a pre-order for one of my books once I have the ebook cover designed. That sets the clock ticking. I have to finish the book (if I haven't already – I usually finish the drafting process before I set up my sales channels), do any revisions, proofread the book, design the paperback cover, format the interior, and set up my launch strategy all before the "dead date" for uploading my files on Amazon.

The times where I haven't done this, or where I have set the release date too far in advance, I have not been productive on finishing. I tend to get the same amount of work done in two weeks as three. There are also multiple books I haven't released as of this writing because I was too afraid to push myself and set up a deadline, so the manuscript sits and waits for my return. I'm sure they'll get released eventually, once I can set up a deadline and therefore a timeline for completion.

Wars Are Won One Battle at a Time

Here is another way of framing the situation without having to think about horses giving birth: **you are waging war.**

You are fighting against the impulse to abandon your projects and avoid the risk of rejection that comes with public display of art. You are fighting against your own need for comfort and rest.

And how is a war won? A single battle at a time.

Every day is a battle. If you lose a single battle, you can still win a war, but the end result of the war is the culmination of the effects of all the battles in it. No general wins a war by losing all of his battles.

If you fail to do your work a single day, it's not a big deal, but the tendency is to let your work slip by day after day, then week after week, until you are no longer creating anything, but engaging in all the other things in life. I've seen this in myself, where I let something go one day, and within a short amount of time, the frequency and quality of my work declines dramatically. I've seen it others as well.

You *have* to be willing to work when you don't feel like working. You absolutely must be willing to make yourself temporarily uncomfortable in order to finish what you have started.

It's kind of like a diet. Eating a donut once a week isn't going to kill you, but eating one (or more) every single day means that you aren't actually on a diet. It's easy to eat a donut every day if you decide you are going to eat one whenever you feel like it. Hell, I feel like eating a donut right now!

The way you are going to avoid falling out of your good work habits is to fight to maintain them. Really muster your self-discipline to work when you don't feel like it, and eventually your process will become a true habit. Then it becomes much harder to lose the battle and therefore the war.

What is Your Cash Crop?

Most farmers these days specialize. They produce a single product in as large a quantity and quality as they can. It wasn't always this way, and farmers in previous periods used to, by necessity, produce a variety of crops. A large, interconnected economy allows for more efficiency through specialization, which has driven the focus toward monoculture. If your land is particularly good for citrus, then there is really no reason to grow crops that aren't as well suited, since you can buy those with your citrus profits.

However, the trend is reversing slightly, at least where I live, because *efficiency isn't always efficient.*

If you have a late freeze, you could lose your citrus crop and go under. If you also grow olives, then you have a safeguard against momentous events for only a little extra effort.

What does this have to do with creativity?

A lot, at least in the current economy.

The contemporary artist must be more than an artist and produce more than art. A novelist must write books, yes, but he must also maintain a social media presence, produce content for a blog or website, and be a marketer for his own work. This is true today whether you are self-published or traditionally published. Other fields are similar. No longer can you focus on your absolute specialty to the exclusion of all else and still find success. It's just like a car manufacturer – it has to do more than just make good cars, it has to get them to customers and convince customers to buy them.

At the same time, you have to be realistic about what your *cash crop* is. What among all the tasks and foci of your profession is the *most* valuable and important thing? This is the thing that you must never be lax on.

Too often I see artists, particularly authors, avoid publishing their work and instead focus on the social media game, even when they only have a social media following *because* of their past publication record.

What is the impetus for this? I think it has to do with gratification. Putting out a social media post or YouTube video gives an immediate sense of impact, importance, and social status. Writing a thousand words that won't be read for months gives none of these things.

What these authors in effect do is spend time pressing their two acres of olives and choosing beautiful bottles for their oil while forgetting to tend to their hundred acres of oranges.

So, returning to the concepts of focus from chapter one, what is your cash crop? For me, it is books, while my side crops are videos, music, blogs, and social media interaction. I can tell you that I personally will have trouble closing twitter on an engaging conversation or avoiding YouTube comments, but this is something I absolutely must do sometimes in order to ensure my cash crop reaches harvest.

After all, people tune in for my writing advice because I write books, not because I happen to have an account on YouTube.

It's good to have a side-hustle or two, but don't get side-tracked.

Be Patient

This is the last, and perhaps the most relevant, analogy for farming: you sow now, you reap later. The quality of your harvest is the culmination of many steps, none of which yield food – that *only* comes at the end.

When you are writing a book, it is worthless until you finish it. This is why I tell new authors to always finish their first draft before trying to do any revision (and of course, always finish what they start). A complete manuscript, even a bad one, is more valuable than anything which is incomplete, however good its parts might be. You have to soldier on and get to your harvest, otherwise, all the planting, pruning, and watering are for nothing.

We all want things now. Success always comes after work. Don't forget this. Don't also forget that the point is to harvest. If you refuse to pick your fruit when it is ripe, it will rot on the vine.

Chapter 7 – Avoid Perfectionism

This is the only chapter of the book focused on a negative, or a "don't" rather than a do. This is for good reason, as *perfectionism* is one of the biggest hindrances to output across all artistic fields. The worst part is that it is a mostly imagined personal flaw, and people are, in my experience, unnecessarily avoidant of publication.

Perfection is Impossible.

Let's tackle the most important point I can make about perfectionism:

You can't be perfect. The things you make can't be perfect either.

We live in a fallen world full of imperfect people, and the things we make are also going to be imperfect. All you can do is your very best with the time and resources that are given to you. And of course, since this is a book about productivity, you cannot have infinite time to complete a project. If that is what you want, you can check out my other book, *Keys to Leaving Things Unfinished Upon Your Death*. I'm not sure when it will be published, but rest assured, when I finally release it, it will be *perfect.*

You might doubt me and my snark. You might point to some piece of art that you consider perfect. If you were to actually ask the artist about it (which you sometimes can, if they are still alive and reachable), chances are they will say that they are happy with it, but won't ever admit to perfection. There's always something that could be done better.

As a performer, I have played live hundreds of times. Perhaps thousands. I've never had a perfect performance in all the years I've spent with my instrument. I've asked some of my favorite performers, some with orders of magnitude more experience than me, and I get the same response: there are good performances, even *best* performances, but no *perfect* performances.

Even if I play every note perfectly for an entire set, there is always something I know that I could have done better. I could have used better phrasing somewhere. I was slightly off of the right tempo for one piece. I didn't perform a crescendo as well as it could be done, or I played with too muddy a tone during a quiet section. There is *always* something.

In one way, this is good, because there is always growth that can happen. In another way, it's maddening, because you are questing for something which cannot be reached.

What's important to focus on is that the process, the journey, is more important than the arrival point (which cannot be reached). You should seek perfection, but know that due to our limited time alive and our limited capacity as mortal beings, you cannot achieve it. The pursuit of the good *is* the good, to put it another way.

Keep in mind that there are aesthetic systems which not only accept imperfection, but view it as something that contributes to the beauty. *Wabi-sabi*, which is one traditional Japanese aesthetic, views imperfection in presentation as reflecting the nature of existence, in that it is both imperfect and impermanent. Contained within the aesthetic is deep meaning – that we are here a limited time, nothing can be truly said to be finished, and therefore nothing can be truly said to be perfect. Imperfections make things unique and interesting.

The art reflects the realities of life.

A western expression of this focus on transience can, I believe, be found in Jazz. Improvisation is the primary defining characteristic of all forms of Jazz, which expresses the moment, rather than being thoroughly composed ahead of time. You gain something from the experience of music being created and fading away within the present by giving up the attempt at the perfection that comes from strict composition. The point of improvisation is the true expression of the music, not so much a perfect selection of notes, otherwise, you would carefully write your melodies ahead of time. This is evidenced in the recordings of the masters. There are many missed notes on those old tapes and records, now immortalized.

It is no coincidence that "Autumn Leaves," a song about transience, is such a popular standard.

You can make excellent art. You cannot make perfect art. Embrace this reality.

Are You Really A Perfectionist?

This might offend you, but chances are that you are not *really* a perfectionist. You are, in all likelihood, similar to most people in that you fear having your work be negatively criticized.

This is natural and is part of being human. Negativity has a bigger impact than positivity, something that goes back to our roots as tribal peoples. In a small tribe, one person hating you can mean your death.

The internet artificially amplifies negativity, removing it from the constraints of a social group that mitigates or suppresses negative interpersonal feelings. Having somebody give you a one-star review on the internet can make you feel the same feelings as if somebody in your tribe hates your contribution to the tribe – but this illusory. There are more opportunities than ever to publish your work and attract an audience, but due to the two-way nature of social media, it is also harder than ever before to avoid negative criticism.

Somebody, somewhere, is not going to like you. Somebody, somewhere, is not going to like your art. The more successful you are, the more people will not like you.

You need to overcome the fear of negative criticism and let people view your art. Working infinitely on revisions will not net you perfection. In fact, you will be avoiding the very process you need to be subjected to so that you *can* get closer to perfection.

When I have a reader say they liked one thing but not another in one of my books, I pay attention. I don't rewrite the book, but I do take note of what had a good effect and what went against my intent for the next project. You continue with your successes and you try to improve on your shortcomings.

If nobody sees your product, you won't know for sure what you did well and what you didn't.

Another truth I have noticed is that, aside from the most hateful people who can't be satisfied anyway, audiences overwhelmingly focus on the positive aspects of a work and forgive its shortcomings, even if they point them out. I've talked to people who love *The Phantom Menace* and say it is one of their favorite movies, while at the same time saying they disliked Jar-Jar Binks.

It's the things you do very well that will make the biggest impact, not *lack* of flaws. Spend a little time putting art out into the world and you will find this for yourself.

Every time you try to do something original and interesting you are taking a gamble that people will hate it. The only real way to avoid flaws it to make something so boring that nobody would notice it, like a perfect steel cylinder. Put a perfect steel cylinder in the middle of a gallery of art, even modern art, and many people will assume it is just a trash can and not give it a second glance. Modern art is ugly, but at least it isn't boring.

What is a *real* perfectionist, anyway?

I define a perfectionist as a person who will refuse to accept a product that does not match his vision of said product perfectly. There are definitely artists and writers who fit this description.

One example that comes to mind is Jari Maenpaä, of the Finnish metal band Wintersun. He waited years to release a promised album called *Time,* then put out only half of the record and refused to release the other half. The reason? He didn't have the resources to make the recording match his vision of it. If you listen to *Time I,* which was released in 2012, you can probably see why. It's a bombastic work of extreme heavy metal, crossing well outside the normal confines of the genre and using layers and layers of non-standard synths and instruments. It's a great recording, truly one of the best I have heard, but that didn't stop Jari from re-mixing the album and re-releasing it digitally as *Time 1.5.*

I actually think the remix is worse than the original, but that only serves to illustrate an important point – the perfection of your vision is not necessarily going to mean perfect acceptance or love from others. Your "perfect" product can still get a one-star review. I don't think Jari cares that much about reviews – I truly think he cares about his album matching his grandiose vision.

If Jari had instead released the complete album – however imperfect when matched to what is going on his head – I think his band would be in a much better position than where it is now, at least as far as notoriety and financial success go (I realize I am talking about a Finnish metal band here, and chances are you know nothing of them). They could have used the lessons from that project to improve the next one. What they ended up doing was crowd-funding a studio by selling yet another album so that Jari could finally produce *Time II* the way it needs to be produced to match his vision.

How many more albums could have been released in the last 15 years had Jari been able to get over his perfectionist nature, or else had been subject to deadlines that would have limited his ability to put off releasing his albums?

Consider this with yourself – would you rather have one perfect book released, or ten imperfect books and an actual career as a writer, knowing that your "perfect" book will not actually be perfect and also still get 1-star reviews?

I strongly encourage you to be prolific rather than perfect. Upping your output will get you closer to perfect than endless revision of a single work.

The Obsession With Revision

I'll let a recent YouTube comment introduce this concept for me (just as an aside, I have nothing against this person, he just represents this perspective rather well):

> Editing and Revisions are the most important
> things you need to face. Any writer who thinks

their stuff is good after the first draft is a delusional idiot and their stuff sucks. Editing, cutting out as much crap as you can after you've written it, is a painful and necessary thing; it's something every writer has to sit down and do with an almost callous seriousness, their story will be better for it. And revisions, many many many revisions, are required to truly make a story good; you are the master of the future and past, you can play revisionist history as much as you need to to make yourself seem like a brilliant writer who had all the steps planned out -- so do that, go back and iron out all the wrinkles and plant all the seeds that will come to beautiful fruition -- don't think that the work you just hammered out is even worth showing to another human being, if you can be bothered to polish it at all then it isn't worth anyone's time to read. Writers who refuse to edit, and don't think that their story needs any revisions, are the worst writers of the most lazy, sloppy, pathetic, festering drivel ... and writers who mindlessly rely on auto-correct/spell-checker, and never bother to look up word definitions and synonyms, are also pathetic and awful. It's either the arrogance, ignorance, or laziness, but those notions/beliefs/habits are possessed by the worst (and most stubborn) writers.

I haven't altered anything in the YouTube comment; let's focus on the prime idea of this message and just keep any emotional reaction in the back of our minds.

I've talked to many professional-level writers over the last few years and listened to many more talk honestly about processes, and the only ones to do revisions on such a scale are screenwriters, and even they have their limits. That's mostly due to the way studios work from script through production, with many eyes making many demands on a final story. This is very unlike other writing mediums where the revision process is 1-2 steps or possibly none at all.

Most authors prefer to do as little work in the revision phase of a book as possible, myself included. My last book contained only a few corrections in the revision phase, and about half the typos were found by readers in the first few days of release (yes, I ship with typos, but so do big publishers, so I usually give myself a pass if I miss only a few). Despite this, it has a 5-star rating on Amazon. It could be that my readers really like me (which I hope they do), or it could be that, considering it was my 11th published book, I knew what I was doing and got the story right on the first try.

Robert Heinlein's *Rules for Writers* had rule #3 as "You must refrain from rewriting, except to editorial order." He didn't create this idly. The belief that you can re-write to perfection is both misguided and a waste of time. Editorial order makes the re-write clear: *this is what needs to change.* It's easy and defined, whereas author-directed editing is often a morass of self-doubt and guesswork on the effect of the story.

I've personally found, mostly with screenplays, that after the second or third draft the product not only stops improving, it gets noticeably worse because it begins to stray further away from the core set of ideas and feelings that created the work to begin with. This is true even with external editorial input guiding the process. Eventually, your revisions will start to restore earlier versions, and then you know you are on a fool's errand.

I also have had talks with other writers as to where this belief in extreme revision comes from. The common answers are *readers* and *amateurs.*

Readers like the idea of a project being a work of extreme passion that the writer spends long, torturous hours to create. Extreme revision is part of this vision of the author and his product as being something special, even superior to normal humanity. They like the idea of the hard-working perfection-ist artist. The reality is that writing is a craft and the more ex-perienced you are with it the better (and more quickly) you can do it, like with most things.

Amateurs tend to think extreme revision is necessary for a work to be good because, honestly, it *is* necessary *for them.* When you first try something, you are probably going to be very bad at it. My first screenplay sucks. My first novel sits in a drawer. My second novel required significant re-writes to make presentable, and I only was able to do the right kind of re-writes after I had written and published several *other* books. For an amateur, their work is always going to fall short of their ideal, because they haven't developed the skills neces-sary to create at their preferred level.

This is why I recommend most authors put their first manuscript away after finishing it and go celebrate the accom-plishment of finishing a book. Then, those authors need to start the next book. That first work will take a lot of revision, but knowing what to revise will probably require the author to grow and have more experience. A short-cut would be to hire a competent editor to tell you exactly what is not working from a reader's perspective and offer fixes, but this is expensive and not usually an option for a true beginner. It's best to learn and grow first, then get that professional help when you are ready to invest in your product. It also improves the feedback and allows the editor to focus on what needs to change, rather than putting him or her in the role of teacher.

Amateurs as readers tend to like the idea of the "slaving artist," who toils at his craft because it makes them think that they could be great artists, too. They can be, of course, not by endlessly revising their first book, but instead by being prolific. The more stories you write, the better you will get at them, so the idea of a contest between a few "perfect" works and many "imperfect" works doesn't make sense. The more pieces you put out, the closer each one gets to perfect, because you are a better artist each time.

Consider that strong emotion in the YouTube comment. People can get *very* psychically attached to their ideas about how things in art ought to be. If you suggest to somebody that a great product can be made outside of their imagined ideal, they get defensive and lash out. In some cases, it's a form of reactionary envy:

If this person doesn't do it this way, then their product must suck!

They must be lying when they say that they didn't do this; he can't just be better than me.

He can't be that good – it must be the editing that saved it.

That last one is frequently said to me regarding the first Star Wars movie – the idea that Star Wars would have sucked had George Lucas not had competent editing from his wife at the time (she was only one of the editors, by the way).

I see these sorts of emotions all the time, and I never have them. I know there are lots of ways to create a work of art, and I judge the final product, not the process absent from the product. If I pay attention to the process, it is only because of what the output is. I also know different people work in different ways. Some writers like to spend more time in revision and draft quickly, avoiding planning. I draft much more slowly, but because of my careful planning, there is usually less for me to do in the revision phase.

Artists should focus on what works for their own process. These are all guidelines, not laws.

Artists should also focus on actually putting their work out.

The False Dichotomy of Quality and Quantity

How many times have you seen a fellow artist say that they prefer "quality over quantity"?

There is no actual competition between these two. In the professional world, you need to produce high quantities of work *and* have it be high-quality at the same time.

People who frame it as a dichotomy are making an excuse for not being productive and expressing their desire for absolution. "If I take a lot of time to finish this project, it's because I'm making it better," is a kind of self-bargaining to resolve inner dissonance.

You should avoid this kind of self-talk, as it will reinforce your feelings of inadequacy over the long-term. Your work will not be universally loved. How crushing will it be to get a one-star review on your book after you took years writing your story? It's probably going to happen. Will you take twice as long to write your next book hoping to avoid another crushing review? What happens when you still get a one-star review even though you "took your time" to an even greater degree?

You need to accept that some people not liking your work doesn't mean that it is low quality. The positive reviews should be where your focus is. Hone your process so that you are better at making the stories you are *good* at.

The same goes for other media. Some people are going to hate your style. No amount of waffling over the details will make them love it.

Also to my point, you may notice that the great artists of both today and yesterday were not only very prolific but also produced a large body of high-quality work. The example has already been set, you need merely rise to meet it.

Generally, output has been the key to mastery. Each completed piece is a step toward greatness. You can't take those steps if you can't work on something, finish it, and let it go.

Chapter 8 – Consume Art

TV and video games are a waste of time, right? Shouldn't timewasters be something you should avoid?

To be fair, leisure activities can be a major time sink if you engage in them rather than do your work, however, they are something that we all need. Everyone needs some downtime to unwind and relax. Everyone needs to be able to enjoy an experience for its own sake.

More than that, as an artist, you need to *dedicate time* to the consumption of art. Your aesthetic sensibilities don't exist in a vacuum where no inputs are needed to produce quality work. Artists need to be experiencing other art to have a sense of what art is supposed to be. A musician cannot create music without having heard music, for example.

So no, TV and video games are not necessarily wastes of time. They are art, which means they can be something necessary for the life of an artist – for inspiration as well as for gaining a deeper appreciation of craft.

I personally struggle with my relationship with media consumption in that I tend to ignore it as a need and spend my time instead on work, or I tend to focus entirely on consuming something and put my work on the back burner. I'm at my best when I actively make time to consume and enjoy art but put it in its proper place in my schedule.

Efficiency isn't always efficient

One of the most important lessons I've learned over the last 20 years is that I cannot have 100% uptime when it comes to productivity. I suspect that nobody can, because I haven't yet met anyone that can, ever. I've only met people who excel at managing their time, not people who can work without any need for leisure.

If I try to have 100% uptime, I get burned out. I can work exceptionally hard for a limited amount of time, say six weeks max (as I've talked about before), but after that time, work starts to become miserable and I long to do something that is fun in and of itself. I'll take a break, read books and play games for a week, then feel anxious that I'm wasting days not progressing toward my goals, and then I end up in an annoying cycle. Sprints shouldn't be a normal state of affairs.

I also notice that when I focus on spending all of my free time working, my cognitive capacity begins to diminish. Although I'm efficient with my time when it comes to maximizing the time during the day spent on work, I'm not being efficient within the time I'm working. My mind starts to drift and slow down. I'll get sleepy, or bored, or feel like my sentences are not flowing from the ether of my mind in the way I'm used to.

Basically, I can't get in the zone when I'm trying to push for maximum uptime.

I've learned this lesson many times in many different capacities over the years, but I keep making the mistake of thinking, "this time, I'm going to put my nose to the grindstone and get it done. No breaks!" It doesn't usually work out, except in short bursts.

I first learned this as a music composition student. Being highly dedicated to productive output even back then, I would force myself to sit at a computer for hours on end and not get much done. I found that if I took a break every hour, even for five minutes, and talked to other students or just read a book in the hallway (always away from the computer), I would be more efficient when I sat down to work. Because of the intensity of my schedule, these breaks were often to the vending machine in the middle of the night, but even then, they were effective.

I liken it to washing off your palette in painting (or cleansing your *palate*, in culinary terms). When you wash the paint off your palette, you have to remix all of your colors for your painting. Removing the drying leftovers of your current set of mixes can make you see what you are doing from a new angle by forcing you to rethink your color choices. In this analogy, the palette is my mind and the colors are the sounds and melodies I am using to create my music.

If I took a break when composing music my mind would stop working on the current problem, like a tough counterpoint section, and new ideas would be free to form in all the layers of my thought. I would find myself energized to get them onto paper.

I relearned this lesson as a performer, finding that if I practiced non-stop for more than about an hour the quality of my practice would rapidly diminish. My focus would be shot, I'd get fixated on the wrong elements, and I would, more than anything, get bored. Doing the same thing – walking out of the practice room and doing something else – would allow my mind to do more total work over the course of a day.

If I had a whole day to write (which I never have now), I found that I had to break up the day into some sort of schedule, or else I would get writer's block – even if I knew what was coming next and had done a lot of story planning. The sentences just wouldn't *flow* from my mind the way they normally do. What was better was writing in one block, then performing some other task such as doing the dishes, then writing in another block, then walking to the store, then writing, then going to the gym, etc. Trying to write for eight hours straight never yielded as many words as writing for four hours and doing other things in between.

Your mind is like a machine

I like to think of the mind, especially with the relationship between consumption (or experience) of art and the production of art, like a car. A car is a complicated machine, and so is your mind. You must maintain and take care of your car, or it will break down. If you don't fill it full of petrol, it will die on you.

With creativity, the art you consume is like the gasoline that you put in your tank. It fills up your mind with possibilities and inspiration, which are then expended when you create. You have to fill up the tank from time to time, or the machine will not work. Likewise, you need to take time to care for the complicated machine that is your mind, a machine that, like an automobile, functions almost magically when in good condition. That means attending to your mental and emotional state is sometimes necessary. You don't stand much chance at creating when you are experiencing intense grief or anxiety.

How you deal with emotional states is up to you, but I think it is generally a mistake to think you can operate at the same level as normal while in an extreme emotional state.

As a side-story, I actually played guitar at my father's funeral, but I was able to do this because I was extremely well-practiced, with years of performance experience in all emotional states under my belt. I wouldn't have attempted it if my father had not asked it of me while he was alive, nor would I have attempted it without the experience I had as a performer at the time. This is not something I would recommend to your typical performer.

I find it's better when in a difficult emotional state to do things that are enjoyable in themselves. For me, that means playing games and reading books. When your machine isn't running well, you need to take care of it and tune it up.

Consuming art is also one of the best things you can do if you are experiencing post-project depression. Movies and books are things that are enjoyable first and foremost, but they also serve to "wash the palette" by filling up the mind with new art, which means new inspirations for new projects. Taking time after completing a large project to enjoy the art you love will remind you of why you got into your field in the first place.

Inspiration is **not** overrated

I used to say inspiration is overrated, because inspiration is not the hard work necessary to complete a project, nor is it the knowledge of the craft that is necessary to make the project good.

As I've matured, I've developed a different perspective and decided that inspiration is incredibly important. It's the impetus to create as well as the destination. Yes, inspiration alone will do nothing for you, and the only way to your goals is through hard, hard work, but do not think that having a deep feeling for what you want to create is something without value.

Anything can inspire, but for me, inspiration has always come at least partially through art – either directly or in how it interacts with my memory and within present moments. *The Water of Awakening,* my first published fantasy novel, was in a large part inspired by the Twilight Force album *Heroes of Mighty Magic,* so much so that I ended up using a painting by Karem Beyit, the band's album artist, for the cover of my book.

It might be surprising for a fan to hear that, given that Twilight Force occupies not only a different medium (music, rather than literature) but also a very different approach within the fantasy genre compared to my work. Their music is pure adventure escapism, like playing *Dungeons and Dragons* or reading Dragonlance books such as *Dragons of Autumns Twilight.* My book (and those that have followed) are much more brooding and philosophical, in the vein of Michael Moorcock. That's who I am, but *Heroes of Mighty Magic* made me feel like I wanted to tell a tale of high adventure, and that is what I did.

To that end, I don't think it is necessary to spend all of your time consuming media that is in the field in which you are working (like books if you are an author), as inspiration can come from anywhere. However, it is important to know your own medium and genre well. You will get to know it by experiencing what other artists have done within it.

Analysis and Acquiring Tools

One of the most important reasons to consume art is to gain the tools to produce your own. You gain these tools by observing what others have done, taking note of how they did things, and learning to use their techniques in your own work in your own way.

If you are an author, pay attention to the prose of the books you read. Take note of the tone, the sentence length, and how much prose there is relative to dialogue. Observe how authors balance plot and character development. Take note of event pacing – how many pages are there between significant events? Even if you don't like a book, you will have gained from the experience if you can understand why you didn't like the book and, perhaps more importantly, why others *did* like it.

Twilight was a fun read for me from this perspective. The prose style of Stephanie Meyer made the main character very relatable and likable – particularly I believe for the target demographic of young teens. There was a great balance between well-timed character interaction that slowly exposed a mysterious character and plot events that propelled the two main characters toward one another. These are lessons that can be applied to other genres to please a wide variety of readers, even though *Twilight* was definitely not the kind of book I would normally choose to read.

Every art experience can offer you something as an artist. Your "artist brain" is something you shouldn't turn off. This was even the case for me when watching movies I considered truly awful, like the recent Disney *Star Wars* movies. Witnessing failure at the least let me know what didn't work and what I didn't want to do with my own art.

One interesting piece of pushback I've received when advocating an analytical approach to art consumption is that looking at something with a critical eye somehow removes the "magic" of the experience. While I personally don't enjoy something less because I understand what techniques are at play, removing the "magic" is precisely the point of analysis. If you want to be an artist, it helps to know what you are doing (unless you are making post-modern art, I suppose, but that is another discussion entirely). You wouldn't expect an engineer to design automobiles without first learning how they work, and you wouldn't accept his desire to view cars as magical steel beasts created by wizards as an excuse for his ignorance.

Artists of all stripes seem resistant to the idea of analysis, but I find that it is particularly bad among musicians. Perhaps it is some combination of the opaque nature of music theory, the fact that a novice doesn't readily understand what is happening in music or why it makes him feel things, and the belief in pure emotional expression in art. The result of resistance to learning music theory is an artist who creates a highly simplistic set of music compositions and who also experiences distress over not being able to imitate the music which inspired him to begin with.

Even highly emotional art, like that of van Gogh, is still full of technique. In his paintings, the technique is even more obvious because he makes no effort to hide his brush strokes.

Analysis is one of the best ways to learn, and I have a YouTube channel heavily devoted to it. From analysis, you extract techniques. With techniques, you can create new art that communicates your message in the manner you envision.

Keep in mind that media like films and games combine multiple disciplines. If you are a musician, a movie has a score that you can analyze. If you are a visual artist, games contain art assets you can evaluate. If you are a writer, movies contain stories and so do most modern games, and thus there are story-telling techniques to glean from them. I should note, however, that these multi-media presentations of art are not going to be the same as the pure version. Watching a movie is *not* the same as reading. Movie and game scores are not composed in the same way stand-alone music is at all, though they may utilize the same music theory concepts. Likewise designing an animated character is not the same as illustrating a static scene.

You still need to know *your* area of expertise.

What writers usually miss in analysis

One of the reasons literature majors don't automatically turn into great writers is that they tend to focus on the wrong things when it comes to analyzing fiction. Most literature classes focus on historically informed readings or the various modern and post-modern forms of criticism (like deconstructive or feminist criticism). They aren't the only ones focusing in the wrong direction. Most analysis content on the web focuses on things like themes, allegory, imbedded messages, prose, and (in genres like fantasy) world-building, and magic systems.

These elements aren't unimportant at all, but they are not what makes a story a good, memorable read. Here are some things writers should focus on instead (in no particular order):

1. Story events. What happens? What order do things happen in? What was unpredictable? What impact did the events have?

2. Dialogue. Readers get attached to characters through dialogue.

3. Character action. Readers love characters by loving what they do.

4. Pacing. Pacing has more to do with the importance of a scene and its tension than it does with the speed of prose.

5. The stakes. This is the core of the main conflict or main plot goal – how does the story matter?

With these five things in mind, I think it is easy to see how a typical reader is going to get bored reading most attempts by new writers at "literary fiction." Personal, "deep" stories often contain low stakes, minimal story events or story events with low importance, an abundance of prose, and many scenes of character interaction that are superfluous to the plot. Great pieces of literature will have those deep elements literature buffs care about, but also be good stories in their own right.

What you focus on when you engage in analysis is just as important as taking the time to analyze in the first place.

Chapter 9 – Break the Rules

When I say, "Break the rules," I also mean the rules of this book. If you read what I have written, consider what I have to say, and then do something completely different that works for you, then this book has done its job. Ultimately, you are on your own path and will have to find your own unique way to accomplish your goals. My guidelines are not universal laws, but rather means of accomplishing project completion in the arts which are time-tested and effective when used by a wide range of people. If something isn't working for you, *try something else.*

I break the rules all the time. I publish my books myself. I design my own book covers – a big no-no if you listen to most author advice (even my own advice – hypocrite that I am). I write whatever I feel like – I don't write to market. I don't edit my YouTube videos.

I break the rules because I know what works for me through experience. I also get a thrill from blazing a trail or doing things outside the norm. I try to write original, effective stories, and though I spend lots of time and effort making content on storytelling techniques, I have never, and will never, follow a strict guide for how to write a story, nor will I follow any method for constructing stories in some ideal way. Each book is an adventure for me, and if I had to write according to *Save the Cat* (a famous screenwriting manual by Blake Snyder) or similar writing manuals, I would exit the profession immediately. If I wanted to follow rules, I'd be driving a truck.

Give yourself the freedom to innovate. Don't worry so much about how things are meant to be done and instead do things the way you need to so that you can get them done. For each project, try something new, whether it is a new approach to your method or a new aesthetic direction in your art. Always growing means always pushing to do something new and interesting, not just for yourself, but for the world.

"Break the Rules" was Arnold Schwarzenegger's second rule from his famous "Six Rules for Success," USC commencement speech. It's hard to deny that he broke all the conventions of Hollywood, from his name and accent to his oversized physique. He believed in himself enough to know that just because nobody had done something before did not mean he could not do it. The "way" of doing things need not be the only way.

This is why I don't get upset if somebody has a different approach than I have. I judge outcomes. If what you are putting out is great, it's great. It doesn't matter that you don't have a neutral thumb position on your guitar neck, or you wrote your book in present tense. It doesn't matter to me if you paint digitally or with cheap craft paint. It doesn't matter if you write your first draft with no prose, just dialogue. If it works, it works – full stop.

Rolling the Dice

The unfortunate truth about creative products is that there is no absolute guarantee of success, and the success you do work for is highly variable. Nobody can perfectly predict what the reception to a given work will be, and they certainly cannot predict the mega-successes - the Harry Potters of the world. There is an element of uncertainty, and therefore chance, with every product you put out to the public.

I have experienced this most profoundly on my YouTube channel, where I can see the dice rolls happening in real-time. I have videos with hundreds of thousands of views, many of them made when I had only a few thousand (or a few hundred) subscribers. I made a Star Wars review in 2015 that ended up blowing up in a big way, making me pay real attention to my YouTube endeavors from that point forward. It was not something I expected at all.

In the follow-up, I thought I could capitalize on that attention, and I did to a certain extent, but random events like that are often singular and difficult to duplicate.

Even when I reviewed *The Last Jedi,* and predicted that it would get some modest attention, the actual attention I got was far beyond my expectations. I've seen the same effect on countless other videos. I throw up a video talking about some random thing on my mind and it will get 10-100 times my normal viewership. Sometimes they get 1000 times my normal viewership!

This perpetuates an unfortunate cycle with most YouTubers. They achieve viral success randomly, then move to capitalize on the attention only to despair when their viewership either slowly drops off or returns to some baseline level. It's not an easy way to make a career, but you will have a better chance at it by knowing what you are going up against.

I've seen random outcomes with my books. *Voices of the Void,* an experimental short sci-fi/horror book I put out in 2019 has ended up being my most popular book by sales, and I have never advertised it. I had expected nobody to like it besides me due to its odd construction. It was presented without any chapter or scene breaks, and the protagonist was the only character who could speak properly – otherwise he was talking to robots and a girl who was mute.

Therein lies part of the key to success. *You have to break the rules.* You can't expect to do the same thing over and over and get different results. You need to be willing to try new things and new variations of old things.

This doesn't mean you should break all the rules all the time. Most mega-successes have one foot in the familiar. *Harry Potter*, for example, is a variation of "mage college" fantasy, much like *A Wizard of Earthsea* by Ursula K. LeGuin, but with an element of escapist portal fantasy (like Edgar Rice Burroughs's *John Carter* books) and a mystery plot. The novelty was in the combination of previously established tropes rather than in pure imagination.

I think that's a good explanation, but a good explanation doesn't convert into a predictive model. If the success of Harry Potter could have been predicted they never would have made Rowling change the name of the first book for the American audience, and they would have been pushing multiple other books just like hers.

Novelty is an important element, perhaps even a necessary element, but it is *not* a sufficient condition for success.

I'm not saying it is all dumb luck, either, just that chance is part of success and is not predictable in the extreme areas of success. You can still write a book to market and reasonably expect to do well with it if you follow the time-tested techniques of good writing and include your best estimation of what readers want. It probably won't be the next Harry Potter, though. To do that, you have to break some of the rules.

The Classroom Mindset

In most western countries, we spend 13 years sitting in a classroom – maybe 20 if you want to get a doctorate.

That's a huge amount of programming directed toward making a person operate the way the institution prefers for him to operate. The result is that people are conditioned to expect and desire certain things, namely clear and sequential instructions.

The problem is, creativity is about working *against* such limitations. After all, if you are painting by numbers you aren't really creating – you are iterating.

I have had many people come to me over the years asking for specific guides for the "correct way" to write a story. They ask for the "rules" of writing (and some authors give them, including Elmore Leonard) and expect that following those rules will deliver them a good story.

They are stuck in the classroom mindset, asking the teacher what they must do for their assignment, what the rules of the classroom are, and especially what things they should *not* do if they want to avoid a lower grade.

The reality of writing books (and I *will* put out a writing manual, sooner or later) is that there is no set of strict instructions, and any "rules" are made to be broken. What you have instead of rules are techniques, which are ways of doing things that you can generally expect to have a certain effect on the reader. Plot formats exist because time has tested certain event sequences and pacing by subjecting audiences to countless variations of them.

Techniques are things that you can use, ignore, or do variations of.

Music theory is another example. The "proper" way to end a song is not a perfect authentic cadence but whatever cadence evokes the effect you desire. A half cadence would leave the listener with a sense of longing, which may be exactly what you want. Non-functional harmony could be what you want, too. You might give them a deceptive cadence to end a little sadly.

You are the artist. You make the rules for your own art, and you get to break whatever rules you want.

You aren't a prisoner of a schoolroom desk anymore. You are a creator!

Don't worry

So this is my final message to you: don't worry about the rules. These are starting places, not ending places. These are paths to get you going on your journey, but where they take you is your decision alone. The final destination should be the completion of your projects. It's up to you to apply your self-knowledge and design the best process to get there.

Actually, I lied. My final message is this:

Thank you for reading my book.

About the Author

David Van Dyke Stewart is an author, musician, YouTuber, and educator who currently lives in rural California with his wife and children.

He is the author of *Muramasa: Blood Drinker, Water of Awakening,* the *Needle Ash* series, *The Crown of Sight, Voices of the Void,* as well as numerous novellas, essays, and short stories. He is also the primary performer in the music project *David V. Stewart's Zul.*

You can find his YouTube channel at http://www.youtube.com/rpmfidel where he creates content on music education, literary analysis, movie analysis, philosophy, and logic.

Sign up to his mailing list at http://dvspress.com/list for a free book and advance access to future projects. You can email any questions or concerns to stu@dvspress.com.

Be sure to check http://davidvstewart.com and http://dvspress.com for news and free samples of all his books.

Made in the USA
Monee, IL
02 May 2020

29433784R00075